EYES OF UNDERSTANDING:
Seeing Life from the Heart-Side Out
By Stephen Shepherd

Copyright ©2021 by Stephen Shepherd (Higher Ground Books & Media) All rights reserved. No part of this publication may be reproduced in any form, stored in a retrieval system, or transmitted in any form, or by any means (electronic, mechanical, photocopying, recording or otherwise) without prior permission by the copyright owner and the publisher of this book.

Scripture taken from King James Bible, Copyright 1990, by Thomas Nelson, Inc. All rights reserved worldwide.

Higher Ground Books & Media
Springfield, Ohio.
http://highergroundbooksandmedia.com

Printed in the United States of America 2021

TABLE OF CONTENTS

CHAPTER ONE
SEEING EVIL IN PLAIN SIGHT

1. Evil as Fun
2. Evil as Business
3. Evil as Dissatisfaction
4. Evil as Conformity
5. Evil as Ambition
6. Evil as Consumerism
7. Evil as Group Think
8. Evil as Monetary Success
9. Evil as Possessions
10. Evil as Good Intent
11. Evil as Normal
12. Evil as Bad Luck

CHAPTER TWO
REASONS TO LIVE IN THE SPIRIT

1. To Understand Life Before It's too Late
2. To Understand Life's Purpose
3. To Fill Life's Void
4. To Establish Moral Boundaries
5. To Avoid Selfishness
6. To Gain Strength

7. To Find Comfort
8. To Find Hope
9. To Understand Sin
10. To Feel Your Need for Jesus
11. To Know Jesus' Healing Power
12. To Know What's Valuable
13. To Protect Your Soul
14. To Find Your Holiness
15. To Find Faith

CHAPTER THREE

30 LIFESTYLE CHOICES TO NURTURE YOUR SPIRITUAL SELF

1. Buy a Bible and Read it Daily
2. Learn to Listen
3. Rethink Money's Importance
4. Don't Hide from God; You Can't
5. Acknowledge the Sin Within You
6. Live Moderately
7. Listen to the Holy Spirit—Jesus' Messenger
8. Remember: Your Salvation Starts Today
9. Know Your Spiritual Ancestry
10. Guard Against Sinful Distractions
11. Control Your Ego
12. Remember: You're A Child of God
13. Live a Spirit-filled Life

14. Believe in Jesus' Supernatural Power
15. Spread the Good News
16. Use Non-Violence
17. Practice Christian Charity
18. Avoid Unchristian Behavior
19. Trust in God and His Son Jesus
20. Do Good Works with Charity
21. Be Generous
22. Fear God's Power
23. Don't Backslide into Sin
24. Believe in Your Holiness
25. Discern Evil
26. Know Your Skills Come from God
27. Don't Worship False Gods
28. Know Moral Behavior Comes from God
29. Remember, The World is Satan's Ungodly Domain
30. Make Moral Decisions

CHAPTER ONE

SEEING EVIL IN PLAIN SIGHT

"Evil does not seem immediately repulsive but may even be seen as attractive on superficial examination, while profoundly destructive at a deeper level." J.R.R. Tolkien, The Hobbit

1. Evil as Fun

Not long ago, my wife and I went with our in-laws to their log cabin in the northern Wisconsin woods for the 4th of July weekend. The log cabin was built by my sister-in-law's grandfather in the 1950's, and it was located on the shores of a pristine lake. The log cabin's interior had a large fieldstone fireplace and log ceiling beams; it reminded me of a rustic log cabin seen in a classic romantic movie.

We arrived at the cabin on July 3rd and were reminded by a visit from a local resident to attend the 4th of July Parade held every year at a village a few miles away. According to her, the 4th of July Parade was the big event of the year with all the local townships celebrating together.

Early the next morning on July 4th, we gathered our lawn chairs and coolers and made the trek to the parade site, which was the Main Street of a local village. We set up our lawn chairs on one side of the street like a thousand or so other people who lined both sides of the one-quarter mile parade route. The parade started with an honor guard of veterans marching while carrying an American flag. They marched in cadence and stopped in front of the American Legion Hall where a woman with a microphone and a loudspeaker on the back of a pickup truck led everyone in the crowd in the saying of the Pledge of Allegiance. When the crowd murmured the Pledge of Allegiance, I looked at the crowd of people dressed in causal t-shirts and jeans lining the street, and most people had their hand over their heart, and for a moment I was touched by the genuine sincerity and the authenticity of the event. This, I thought, was how real Americans out in the Northwoods celebrate July 4th.

Then, the fire trucks appeared blasting their horns and exacting the shrill of their sirens to the delight of hundreds of kids who lined the parade route. As the fire trucks passed, firefighters tossed tons of candy from the fire truck's windows, and kids scurried beside the fire trucks picking up the candy falling onto the edge of the asphalt pavement.

After many gleaming red fire trucks had driven passed, the floats from the local business organizations appeared. Local church members sat on the first float, which was a flat-bed trailer pulled by a black pickup truck driven by the pastor, who threw candy out the truck window like there was no tomorrow. Then, behind the church float, another curious float appeared. At first, I didn't know what business or organization the float represented, and I leaned over to ask my sister-in-law; she didn't know either. It was then that someone nearby in the crowd clued us in. It was the float from the local strip club. I won't tell you the name of the strip club indicated by a huge sign on the float; it is too crude to mention, but a flat-bed trailer had been "tricked out" with a brass pole, and eight women—the actual strippers—were dancing and waving to the crowd. Most of the strippers carried a long-barreled water gun that shot long streams of water at the crowd. When someone in the crowd was hit by the water, the crowd laughed and cheered. We need not get into what the long-barreled squirt guns symbolized.

By then, I was stunned by the strip club float's presence in the parade and thought: Why does a strip club have a float in a Fourth of July Parade? Who issued them a parade permit? And why is the crowd so accepting of it? And how will parents explain the half-naked dancers on the strip club float to their kids when they get home from the parade? These and many other questions entered my mind, and then suddenly the parade was no longer a wholesome American event but a crude, ugly, and surreal one.

So, why didn't this town consider the inappropriateness of the strip club's float as something more than just "light-hearted fun" as the cheers of the crowd suggested? The answer to the question lies in Satan's skill at masking evil as fun in plain sight, and this distortion often blurs the line between moral and immoral behavior.

1 Corinthians 13:12 states, "For now we see through a glass darkly..." which means that everything in the world is distorted by Satan. In the 4th of July Parade, Satan had successfully distorted crude and immoral behavior as harmless fun. In the world, Satan often suspends moral judgement with the wink-and-nod excuse of being entertained. Unfortunately, many people seem to accept Satan's interpretation of living in the moment instead of thinking about the long-term, moral

implications of their behavior. For them, the instant sensual gratification of the moment is more appealing than thinking about its appropriateness.

And frankly, the sensory impressions in Satan's world are very seductive. If you live your life like there is no tomorrow, then you don't have to think about the impact of what you're doing today. Being unbound by the moral restrictions of your actions can be very appealing. If you accept Satan's premise that a moral boundary doesn't exist, then moderation and judgement don't apply. In Satan's world, unrestricted immoral behavior almost always deletes the restriction of moral judgement.

2. Evil as "Just" Business

"How nice—to feel nothing, and still get full credit for being alive." Kurt Vonnegut, Slaughterhouse-Five

I once knew a married couple who owned a lucrative corporation that manufactured different types of bags. One of their product lines was manufacturing sandbags, and every Sunday they went to church at 8:00 am, sat in the front pew, and prayed like maniacs for a disaster to happen. They prayed for a torrential flood so that they could sell more sandbags. They also prayed for more boots-on-the-ground wars because then they could really make a profit by charging the US Army double the price for a sandbag. Thus, when wars broke out and troops were deployed, they supported our troops by price gouging the US military. Obviously, Satan had convinced this married couple that business profiteering from the misery of others was okay. "But they that will be rich fall into temptation and a snare, and into many foolish and hurtful lusts, which drown men in destruction and perdition" (1 Timothy 6:9). For Satan, it was a Super Bowl win! He compromised the morals of the married couple who made and sold the sandbags, and at the same time he created more misery in the world for hundreds of thousands of people in the war zones.

When a war ended, the sandbag couple bought a new yacht with their profits earned by selling sandbags at inflated prices, and then they sailed their yacht around the world visiting the same Third World Countries where the wars had been fought. One time while traveling in the Congo, the couple spotted some of their unused sandbags stacked high on an abandoned pier, so they confiscated the sandbags and had them shipped back to the US to sell them again, probably to the same country where only a fragile peace settlement existed. "He that loveth silver shall not be satisfied with silver; nor he that loveth abundance with increase: this is also vanity" (Ecclesiastes 5:10). Although the people who lived in the war-torn countries were homeless, starving, and human sticks in the dust, their plight didn't register on the moral sensibilities of the sandbag couple. Satan had created an evil barrier of greed in their steely hearts against compassion, thus making the sandbag couple emotionally immune from a human response; for them, war was "just" business.

Years later, I told this sandbag story to an acquaintance of mine who drove a potato chip delivery truck, and he related an immoral business story of his own about Satan's influence on him. One day, a new potato chip brand appeared on his delivery truck along with specific instructions from the manufacturer about how to display the chip bags in the store. Although it was a new potato chip brand, the manufacturer had bribed the US distributors to secure the best eye-level spot on the shelf. In addition, the instructions on how to market the new potato chip brand contained a curious point. The first bulleted point on the marketing instruction sheet for the delivery person told him to take a pin and to poke a pin hole into all the other bags of potato chips, thus rendering their competitors' potato chips stale. When customer complaints quickly flooded onto the store manager's desk about having bought stale potato chips found in the competitors' bags, the managers quickly stocked more bags of the new brand of chip.

Satan probably laughed until he cried over this potato chip story because for him it was another Super Bowl win. First, he had all the marketing personnel at the new potato chip headquarters agree to sabotage the chip bags of competitors. Then he got the distribution headquarters to accept a bribe. Then, he got the distributor's truck drivers to prick pin holes in the bags, and then he got the store managers to believe that the only fresh chip on the rack was the newest brand. Of course, the newest potato chip brand was probably not the best tasting potato chip on the store's rack. But Satan's deceit made it appear to be the best, and that's how deceit in Satan's world works; it seems to always involve a cascading immoral cause and effect relationship where all participants cooperate to collude in an evil and dishonest way. None of the apparent deceit in the potato chip story would have happened if all parties involved had not cooperated because of greed. My acquaintance received an extra $100.00 a week for an entire year for his sabotaging efforts, that is, until the stores removed the other potato chip brands from their shelf. He said that he felt kind of guilty about doing it, but he needed more money. "That no man go beyond and defraud his brother in any matter: because that the Lord is the avenger of all such, as we also have forewarned you and testified. For God hath not called us unto uncleanness, but unto holiness" (1 Thessalonians 4:6-7).

Therefore, while some people living under Satan's thumb in the world might not believe in his moment-by-moment involvement in their everyday lives; in truth, he is there. If you look behind every action in Satan's world, you'll find money and greed. The Bible states in Timothy 6:10 "For the love of money is the root of all evil" because Satan uses money as his primary tool to increase people's immoral and errant behavior. In fact, greed is the most powerful tool in Satan's toolbox; he just loves to plug greed into people's minds to electrify and amp up evil thoughts, and then he just stands back and watches people's greedy behavior subvert their moral values. Over time, greed eventually grinds moral behavior to a pulp. Therefore, because everything in life does directly or indirectly involve money and because people are susceptible to Satan's influence about it, it is likely that Satan is standing nearby you each day to influence your every monetary decision. Even your smallest decision has both a monetary and a moral component. Large or small—in everything you do—Satan is there whispering in your ear and playing tug-of-war with your conscience to use money in selfish ways to undermine the moral authority that God has put into you.

Therefore, Satan is real and has a real presence in your life. It is not paranoid to think that Satan is nearby and that he is trying to influence your decisions; it is simply the truth. From illegally putting too many trash bags into the container for city trash pickup to letting your dog roam in the vacant lot next door to do his "business," the battle for your soul continues between God and Satan in even the smallest events in your life. Contrary to popular belief, the war for your soul being waged between God and Satan is not being fought on one big battlefield. Instead, it is being fought in little skirmishes when you make seemingly innocuous decisions where the small moral choices eventually added up to a sum of your moral character. When you side with God, it will add to your moral character, and when you side with Satan, it will subtract from your moral character. Satan's over-arching strategic goal is to weaken your moral resolve over time by whittling down your moral character one shaving at a time. "Lo, this only have I found, that God hath made man upright, but they have sought out many inventions" (Ecclesiastes 7:29). Therefore, Satan's existence on earth means that living in a spiritual body while existing in a physical one can be very unpleasant experience because your spiritual body is continually being assaulted by Satan's trials. The good news is that God has given you the free will to make the correct moral decisions. In short, whether you do good in the world or whether you do evil is up to you.

Years ago, as young English Instructor at a small college, I experienced first-hand how some people want evil business to happen in Satan's world. The small college where I taught had hired a new English Department Chairperson, and at our first meeting, he had introduced me to his wife. At that time other more pressing academic matters intervened, and the new English Department Chair had to exit my office, leaving his wife alone with me. I could still hear the new English Department Chairperson's footsteps disappearing down the hollow marble hallway when his wife said to me, "Don't get to comfortable behind that desk; I'm going to have your job in two years." Since the moment she uttered this statement, her main evil business goal in life was to get me fired so that she could take my job. It didn't matter to her that I was a good teacher; Satan was directing her actions. From that moment forward, my every good action on behalf of the school and the students was distorted by her to be bad. Gossip, lies, and rumors about me filled the school's hallways and the administration's ears, until two years later, after having done superior teaching and administrative work, I was fired from my job and she was hired to replace me. From this evil incident, I learned that Satan does, indeed, seek to control people's actions and that he is void of moral content, but exists only in every moment as pure and ruthless evil and that it is the job of God's people to fight him. "Be strong and of a good courage; be not afraid, neither be thou dismayed: for the Lord thy God is with thee whithersoever thou goest" (Joshua 1:9).

When I told this story of her evil business plan to get my teaching job to a friend of mine, he related to me his own introduction to people wanting evil business to happen in Satan's world. At the time, he was the vice-president at a small liberal arts college, and a new president had been hired. On Friday morning before the new president's swearing-in ceremony on Saturday morning, the new president gathered the college's five vice-presidents together in a meeting room to announced that he would not be making any new changes to the staff and that all five vice-presidents would be retained. On Saturday morning after the president's swearing-in ceremony, the new president convened another meeting of the vice-presidents and fired them all. When my friend reminded the new president of what he had said on the previous day about retaining all the vice presidents, the new president simply said, "That was then, and this is now." Apparently, the new president had needed the cooperation and the votes of the vice-presidents to get elected to the job; and after the new president had been sworn in, things had changed. "Beware lest any man spoil you through philosophy and vain deceit, after the tradition of men, after the rudiments of the world, and not after Christ" (Colossians 2:8).

As mentioned previously, some people don't believe that Satan exists or that his evil influence is pervasive in their lives; however, any person searching to live with God in their spiritual self instead of living with Satan in their physical self should be prepared for a full-blown attack from Satan. When you reject Satan and put on the moral cloak of the Lord Jesus Christ, Satan will notice you for sure, and he will make a special effort to go after you to revert you back to your own sinful physical self. Therefore, Satan likes nothing better than pinning a bullseye on the back of an aspiring Christian; he takes special delight in walking a Christian backwards down memory lane to view their previous sinful behavior as fun. "Now the just shall live by faith: but if any man draw back, my soul shall have no pleasure in him" (Hebrews 10:38). So spiritual seekers take warning: Once you begin your quest to know more about your spiritual self by listening to the Holy Spirit calling to you as sent to you by the Lord Jesus Christ, you can expect Satan's wrath and darkness to surround you. Yet, you must stand firm in the Lord against Satan. Ephesians 6:10-12 states it best. "Finally, my brethren, be strong in the Lord, and in the power of his might. Put on the whole armour of God, that ye may be able to stand against the wiles of the devil. For we wrestle not against flesh and blood, but against principalities, against powers, against the rulers of the darkness of this world, against spiritual wickedness in high places."

3. Evil as Dissatisfaction

"Better is little with the fear of the LORD than great treasure and trouble therewith" (Proverbs 15:16).

When you play by Satan's rules in the world, you are always running uphill. A Satan-controlled world is only concerned with furthering evil, and your spiritual self is constantly being told to make an immoral choice. Evil is in us and evil demons are all around us in the world, and many people in the world have succumbed to Satan's influence. For instance, every day Satan loves to promote unhappiness through dissatisfaction. Therefore, every time you become pleased and happy with something, Satan will intervene and make you discontent with it. However, James 5:10-11 explains who gives us our happiness. "Take, my brethren, the prophets, who have spoken in the name of the Lord, for an example of suffering affliction, and of patience. Behold, we count them happy which endure."

For instance, let's us say that one day Satan convinces you to buy a new boat that you can't afford. Eventually, Satan will also make that boat become out of style and then whisper in your ear the thought of buying a newer boat. So, you buy a newer and bigger boat, and then Satan makes the newer boat shrink in size so that it appears to be too small, so Satan whispers in your ear the thought that you need to buy a bigger boat. So, you buy a bigger boat. Then, one day Satan makes you look out your living room window to see your next door neighbor's new boat setting in his driveway, and his boat is even bigger and even more luxurious than your boat, so Satan whispers in your ear the thought that you need to compete with your neighbor's boat by buying a newer and more luxurious boat. Thus far, Satan's whispers of "buy a better boat" have just taken 15 years off your life and have deep-sixed your bank account. This is a simple example of how Satan's cyclic mind game works because he has convinced you that buying a newer and better boat will somehow make you a newer and better person, when just the opposite is happening. The truth is that you have just been manipulated and used by Satan to do his will. You are not the winner in the boat buying competition. How could you be? You couldn't even afford to buy the smallest and cheapest boat in the first place. "Let your conversation be without covetousness; and be content with such things as ye have: for he hath said, I will never leave thee, nor forsake thee" (Hebrews 13:5).

The social, economic, and political systems of earth are temporarily controlled by Satan. Therefore, when you let him, Satan will screw up your life big time by ruining both your moral self-control and the bottom line of your bank account. "Not that I speak in respect of want: for I have learned, in whatsoever state I am, therewith to be content" (Philippians 4:11). Of course, some people don't believe that Satan is real and that his demons are intent on destroying their lives. But then, why wouldn't Satan be real? The earth is temporarily his home, and you're living your life in his front yard. If you don't think Satan's demons are lurking in the shadows and trying to influence your decisions, just think about how many times per day you are bombarded with commercial messaging. Satan's commercial messaging to buy something in the digital age is relentless, and Satan's demonic evil rides on the airwaves of every commercial ad. Don't be fooled; it isn't "just business" to get you to buy something; it's Satan controlling your mind to buy it. "For the grace of God that bringeth salvation hath appeared to all men. Teaching us that, denying ungodliness and worldly lusts, we should live soberly, righteously, and godly, in this present world" (Titus 2:11-12).

4. Evil as Conformity

"To be yourself in a world that is constantly trying to make you something else is the greatest accomplishment." —Ralph Waldo Emerson, On Being Yourself

The "piling on" scenario in Satan's physical world suggests that multiple people imitating evil makes doing it okay and that more people should be doing it too. Of course, "piling on" is a football analogy derived from the players' actions on a football field where someone tackles an opposing player and he falls to the turf, only to be tackled again and again by players who continue to pile onto him. This results in a lot of action and drama, as if something important has taken place, but in truth the first tackle completed the job and the subsequent tackles were unnecessary. This analogy mirrors life on Satan's earth. One person does something evil, and suddenly other people are doing it too. The evil action doesn't have to be worthwhile or meaningful; in fact, the more stupid the action, the greater the likelihood that more people will do it too (e.g., the people cheering for the strip club float).

In Acts Chapter 19 when Paul travels to Ephesus, he encounters the artisans in a battle for their souls by conforming to make a moral or immoral decision. It is a good example of the age-old battle of conforming to what others do instead of thinking for yourself and doing what is morally right. In Paul's time, the combatants were the believers in Jesus Christ and the nonbelievers. Satan's secular interests—like ours today—are easier to discern than our more important spiritual interests. In Ephesus, it was a question of making a living in a false way. The silversmiths of Ephesus were making a living by constructing silver images of the goddess of the forest Diana. It was a good living and they did not want their livelihood threatened by Paul and his undermining the goddess Diana with his proclamations about Jesus Christ. For the silversmiths, the decision was an evil no-brainer; they would conform and pile on together and keep Diana as their idol to worship and thus keep their livelihood. Whether the silversmiths believed in the goddess, who knows? But one thing was for sure, other people did by piling on and paying good money for the Diana trinkets that the silversmiths made. "For a certain man named Demetrius, a silversmith, which made silver shrines for Diana, brought no small gain unto the craftsmen; Whom he called together with the workmen of like occupation, and said, Sirs, ye know that by this craft we have our wealth" (Acts 19:24-25).

The silversmiths' perspective is a rational secular one: Why should we give up a good living for our physical selves by trusting in an unknown spiritual entity—Jesus Christ—who promised nothing in this world? For the silversmiths, Satan's here-and-now perspective was much more important than the spiritual hereafter perspective. "… this our craft is in danger to be set at nought; but also that the temple of the great goddess Diana should be despised" (Acts 19:27). This here-and-now secular perspective is shared by people today, who would rather compromise their soul for secular profit and financial gain.

I have often wondered if there was one silversmith in Paul's time who heard the calling of Jesus Christ in his heart and stopped creating the false promises of Diana through the trinkets he made. Did one silversmith take a moral step to think for himself and walk towards

Jesus, even though it would cost him his livelihood? Even today, morally courageous people like these are hard to find; people who place their integrity and moral character before their job are few. Usually, when faced with the battle of spiritual (moral) vs secular (immoral) interests, most people know what they should do, but they often don't do it because Satan convinces them that it easier to do otherwise. Instead of doing what is morally right, they look at their shoes, shuffle their feet, and try to convince themselves that their secular immoral decision was the correct choice.

Years ago, I was hired to teach English composition at a small college. The only stipulation in my contract was that the school controlled which textbooks that I used in my classes. Many schools chose which textbooks instructors used, although at many other schools the professors chose the textbook themselves. On my first day at work and a few days prior to the start of the academic semester, I received a copy of my new textbook from the bookstore, and I noticed that the English Department Chairman was the author. I checked with the bookstore and discovered that the Department Chairman's textbook was the only textbook being used in all 15 composition classes and that I was required to use it. Years ago, the English Department Chairman had self-published a composition textbook and had made its use mandatory at the college. In addition, the textbook was a small paperback and not very comprehensively written. And to make matters worse, the textbook was terribly overpriced. Therefore, the students were required to buy this bad textbook at the inflated price, thus earning the English Department Chairman a considerable textbook royalty every semester. When I went to the bookstore to order another textbook besides the Department Chairman's textbook, the bookstore manager denied my textbook request, and I was told to take up the issue with the English Department Chairman, who had hired me just two months earlier. When I spoke to the English Department Chairperson about the immoral implications of making money by selling his textbook to students at inflated prices and by requiring all instructors to use it, he became defensive and told me that everybody does it and to use the textbook in my classes or quit my job. "For they loved the praise of men more than the praise of God" (John 12:43). Whereupon, I quit my job, which surprised him, but apparently not enough for him to allow me to use another textbook. Before I left his office, I told him that he should be ashamed of himself for using the English Department Chairmanship to exploit the students for monetary gain. But rather than respond to my accusation, he told me to get out of his office and then looked at his shoes and shuffled his feet.

Jesus saves people one person at a time, and no two people will be given the identical set of circumstances in their lives to decide who they will rely upon more—Satan or the Lord Jesus. It is, of course, easier to keep your spiritual-self quiet during the debate over what to do and to choose job security over your spiritual security. However, "Two Roads Diverged in a Yellow Wood"—a poem by Robert Frost—states that the more difficult road to take and moral choice to make is ultimately more rewarding. "I took the one (path) less traveled by, and that has made all the difference."

Therefore, if you perpetually side with Satan and choose your own secular interests over the strength of your own moral and spiritual well-being, it is a dangerous path. For, each time you choose to conform to Satan's secular self instead of God's spiritual self, you dig yourself a deeper moral and secular grave to climb out of at the end of your life. Jesus states, "For this people's heart is waxed gross (callous), and their ears are dull of hearing, and their eyes they have closed; lest at any time they should see with their eyes and hear with their ears, and should understand with their heart, and be converted, and I should heal them" (Matthew 13:15). Eventually, if you side with Satan, you've invested so much more into your secular self that you can't even recognize your spiritual self anymore. Remember: Living in Satan's physical and secular self is a short-term earthy solution and that living in Jesus' spiritual self is a long-term heavenly solution. Jesus states "But ye shall receive power, after that the Holy Ghost is come upon you: and ye shall be witnesses unto me both in Jerusalem, and in all Judaea, and in Samaria, and unto the uttermost part of the earth" (Acts 1:8). So, what good does it do for a silversmith to make trinkets to Diana, yet lose his soul to Satan and go to hell? Every day, I read in the news about people who have sold their souls to the devil by conforming to his evil because they don't have the moral courage to do what is right by Jesus Christ. This is a very dangerous way to live one's life; the money earned and the trinkets bought today in the secular world will have no currency in the next world, unless it is to prove how wrong you were in making so many bad choices." Take heed, brethren, lest there be in any of you an evil heart of unbelief, in departing from the living God" (Hebrews 3:12).

5. Evil as Unholy Ambition

"By faithfully working eight hours a day you may eventually get to be boss and work twelve hours a day." –attributed to Robert Frost

Of course, Satan always makes it easier to conform to the secular crowd than to think for yourself spiritually. He knows that sheep will follow sheep. When the Bellwether sheep—the lead sheep with the bell around its neck—moves, then the other sheep will follow it. The ringing bell around the sheep's neck, of course, was placed there by the sheepherder, who had wisely determined that if he could train all the sheep to follow one sheep, then he wouldn't have to chase after all the sheep himself. Sheep, of course, unthinkingly follow the sound of the bell, no matter what. The Bellwether sheep in Satan's physical world now exist in human form in every part of the globe; they seek followers to do Satan's bidding in behaviors unbecoming of human dignity to satisfy their own need for adulation, and unthinking human sheep who follow them are never in short supply. The Bellwether sheep in human form don't care about your welfare; they only care about their own. "Pride goeth before destruction, and a haughty spirit before a fall" (Proverbs 16:18). The Bellwether type of person always considers himself in charge of others and wants to control their behavior. Dictators are prime examples of Bellwether sheep because they presume to hold power without moral authority.

Many years ago, I mopped the tile hallways in the student union as an undergraduate student. I worked 20 hours per week, usually four hours a day from 5pm to 9 pm. I was single and living in the dormitory at the time, and one night while mopping the tile floors, which extended for miles, I was joined by a young woman who suddenly started talking to me. She was average company, and suddenly she was appearing every night and following me around on my nightly mopping of the floors. Her joining me occurred for about two weeks when a dormitory friend spotted her talking to me one night. After work, I went back to the dormitory where I was met by a room full of dormitory guys waiting for me. The dormy who had spotted me talking with the girl suddenly blurted, "Do you know who the girl is following you around at work?" I replied, "No, who is she?" "She is so-and-so, and she is worth $250 million. How did you get to meet her?" "I don't know," I replied. "She just started following me around at work." "Are you stupid?" he yelled. "Ask her out on a date!" "But we really don't have that much in common," I responded. "For $250 million," he said, "you can learn to love her."

The next day at work, the woman appeared once again and joined me while I mopped the floors. That night, I asked her out on a date, and the next night I arrived at her dormitory room to take her out. And that's when I met her roommate, who went to school with student loans and was deep in student debt, but we made an instant connection, so I started to date her instead. Since then, I have always wondered about people who marry for reasons of unholy ambition instead of love. In fact, the guy who encouraged me to date the wealthy young woman who followed me around while I mopped the student union floors eventually contrived to meet, date, and marry the wealthy woman himself. He wanted to own his own hobby store someday, and he figured that he could get his dream to come true by marrying the girl. The last I heard of them, they were divorced, and he had lost his hobby shop in the divorce settlement. She had moved to the south of France to get a good tan, and he had moved into the shadows of his parents' basement; I guess she must have discovered Satan's evil ambition in him. "Be not wise in thine own eyes: fear the LORD, and depart from evil" (Proverbs 3:7).

Satan controls so many ambitious people on earth by blocking their communication with their Holy Spirit to make them spiritually blind. In Satan's world of mass production and communication where the controlling evil of unholy ambition is celebrated, it is difficult to maintain a sense of decency and individuality. Yet, this is what a person "called" by Jesus Christ through the Holy Spirit is supposed to do. "Howbeit when he, the Spirit of truth, is come, he will guide you into all truth … "(John 16:13). In a world where Satan promotes the illusion that somehow unholy ambition and doing wherever it takes to succeed is good, unholy ambition usually strips away individual moral identity. Satan knows that people are afraid of failure and of being shunned by their peers, so he creates the artificial illusion of worldly success and its acceptability predicated on everyone being ruthlessly ambitious.

However, the ruthless ambitious mantra of Satan's secular world and its controlling allure of success is a far cry from the Christian spiritual perspective of remaining a caring and thoughtful person. A person who has been "called" by the voice of Jesus Christ through the Holy Spirit within them must have the courage to oppose Satan's secular influences. "That which is born of the flesh is flesh; and that which is born of the spirit is spirit." (John 3:6). A called person of God is not a sheep who listens and responds to the collective whims of Satan's controlling ambitions in the world. Satan's bell might ring in most people's ears, but it does not ring in a Christian's ear because they are a spiritual follower of Jesus Christ!

6.   Evil as Consumerism

"Thus, it is that we always pay dearly for chasing after what is cheap." Aleksander Solzhenitsyn, The Gulag Archipelago

In Job 5:7 "Yet man is born unto trouble, as the sparks fly upward" reminds us of the difference between our worldly and spiritual existences. Wouldn't it be nice if we, as Christians living our spiritual lives, didn't have to contend with the friction of Satan's physical world and his evil systems that control it? Yet here we are in it, and that friction is set in stone by God because we are born in a spiritual body but endure life in our physical body on earth. Some people, however, don't believe that their life comes from God and that His spirit is in them. They seem satisfied with embracing the secular world of Satan and the notion that we have all just climbed out of the evolutionary slime to become human. But Job 5:8 reminds us of our Christian spiritual perspective—that we are God's creations and we should be obedient to Him. "I would seek unto God, and unto God would I commit my cause" (Job 5:8).

Of course, this is where the friction begins and where the sparks start to fly. God's spiritual world and Satan's physical world are difficult to reconcile; it seems that you either live in one or you live in the other. The sparks fly when you try to live in both worlds at the same time because they are mutually exclusive. For example, Satan's physical world cares about what people think of you, and God's spiritual world believes that what people think of you doesn't matter. The only judgement that matters to the Spirit is God's judgement. Therefore, all Satan's earthly beauty products and fashion designer clothes don't mean anything to God; they are only the devices of Satan's to make you seemingly look more physically appealing to other people. If God's spiritual world cares about the physical body at all, it is only in terms of it housing the Holy Spirit. Yet, while it does hold the Holy Spirit, the physical body might as well be healthy and clean. So, are you living a healthy lifestyle in caring for God's temple—you? As God hath said in 2 Corinthians 6:16,"… for ye are the temple of the living God; as God hath said, I will dwell in them, and walk in them; and I will be their God, and they shall be my people." And although a clean and healthy body doesn't make a clean soul, God likes cleanliness, and if your physical body carries around your God's presence in your soul, it might as well be clean and healthy. Personally, I avoid expensive and superficial beauty products like creams, hair moose, body gels, and designer deodorants. God made you without these preparations, so you shouldn't automatically buy them and support Satan's argument about their worth or necessity.

Also, secular employment is necessary to earn money to buy food to keep your physical body healthy, but food—according to God—is not a designer contest. How food is plated doesn't matter to God; how nutritional food is for you is what is important to God. Otherwise, why would God have naturally and organically provided all the nutritionally excellent fruit and vegetables without preservatives? By contrast, other types of invented, processed foods don't grow naturally in God's soil. I have yet to see marshmallows growing on a marshmallow tree. In fact, I don't even know what comprises a marshmallow or, for that matter, what's in a cheese product that doesn't contain any cheese, yet Satan wants you to like and to buy them.

In addition, you are not what you wear, so don't buy into Satan's cycle of wearing designer clothing. It is just Satan's excuse for profiteering manufacturers to charge you more money under the illusion of making you appear more socially acceptable to other people. In my opinion, clothes are clothes; pants are pants; shirts are shirts, and socks are socks. Whether they are suitable for the climate is really the question. Therefore, practical clothing that keeps you warm in the winter and cool in the summer is what matters to God. What doesn't matter to Him is how much you paid for it or what manufacturer's tag is on it. That's what Satan wants you to believe. Besides, with global economics blurring the world into one garment manufacturing district, most designer-labeled products are produced cheaply in poverty-stricken

Third World Countries, and by buying them you are participating in Satan's human-chain of exploitation of those people who make them. In short, the clothing that you pay a lot of money for with a designer label is probably no better than other non-designer clothing like it. It's the illusion of being trendy and a better product created by media advertising, not a superior product. Henry David Thoreau said it best in Walden Pond, "Most of the luxuries, and many of the so-called comforts of life, are not only indispensable, but positive hindrances to the elevation of mankind" (Walden's Pond, Economy).

Therefore, every time anyone makes a monetary and consumer decision, they are tempted by Satan to make a worldly choice instead of a spiritual choice. As you can see, in Satan's fallen world the choices we make in even the smallest of decisions reflect either a secular or spiritual worldview. And where conflicting decisions are present, there will always be moral friction. For instance, you are not defined by what type of car you drive. The hood ornament will not give you your next breath. Only God can do that. So, what good is it to be influenced by Satan into driving a car that you can't really afford and that hurts the environment, when you could have purchased a reliable, cheaper, and environmentally friendly car instead? Therefore, when you change from living in your physical self to living in your spiritual self, it changes how you live and for whom you live (Jesus), and this will always create a tension. Satan is real; look around you at the perversion in our world that says wrong is right, and right is wrong. Choosing to live a spiritual existence or a secular existence converges in everyone's life because the two perspectives can't co-exist. Your job, as a spiritual being of God living in Satan's fallen world, is to know the difference between accepting and living in Satan's physical world of idolatry or elevating your perspective about life by living in God's spiritual world. "These things I have spoken unto you, that in me ye might have peace. In the world ye shall have tribulation: but be of good cheer; I have overcome the world" John 16:33).

7. Evil as Group Think

"Like all men who are fundamentally of the group, of the herd, he was incapable of taking a strong stand with the inevitable loneliness that it implied." F. Scott Fitzgerald, Case of Benjamin Button

When you start to listen to your Holy Spirit and to live your life in spiritual terms according to Jesus Christ, you will start to see the illusion of Satan's evil world that herds people into thoughtless and immoral action. If you were born to follow in a group, then you would have all been born in a group, maybe 8 to 10 people born at a time like in a litter of people. Instead, most people are born as a single person with different attributes, attitudes, and perspectives. But you wouldn't know it by Satan's influence on the world of group think and its influence on knowing more than God. If you don't think like me says Satan's world, then you cannot be like me. If you don't look like me, then you cannot be like me. And, if you don't talk like me, then you cannot be like me. "If we say that we have no sin, we deceive ourselves, and the truth is not in us" (1 John 1:8). You get the point. It is easier to define yourself and to be accepted by others if you submit to Satan's world of group think pressure. However, the drawback in joining Satan's group think cadre is that your precious individuality gets lost in the sameness swamp of group-think mentality. In Satan's world, group-think sameness is celebrated as wonderful because it makes all your decisions for you. Yet, eventually your individual soulful self will slowly disappear, and you will slip back into your place in line as an accommodating creature of Satan. "And be not conformed to this world, but be ye transformed by the renewing of your mind, that ye may prove what is that good, and acceptable, and perfect, will of God" (Romans 12:2).

When I was in graduate school, I took an Ethics in Education class with fifty other teachers. Most of the students were in the graduate education program and earning their Masters' Degree in Education. It was a summer school course, so many teachers from the surrounding area were enrolled. After enrolling in the class, I discovered that the regularly scheduled professor had taken a sabbatical so another visiting professor would be teaching the class. The Visiting Professor was working on her Ph.D. from a prestigious university in New York. It was obvious from the start of the class that she was young and ambitious, but because she was teaching an ethics course to educators, I at least expected her to be fair. Yet, during the second week of class, she assigned all fifty teachers in the class an individual topic for their 40-page research paper. Ironically, all 50 topics that she assigned were directedly related to the research that she needed for her own Ph.D. dissertation. In short, she required the fifty professional educators in the class to do her Ph.D. research for her. "And we know that we are of God, and the whole world lieth in wickedness" (1 John 5:19). After I looked on-line to confirm her Ph.D. dissertation topic, I confronted her in her office about her individually choosing our research paper topics, especially when the topics were so related to completing her own Ph.D. dissertation research. I related that it was particularly offensive because her actions were also being done in a class about ethics. She responded nonchalantly with Satan's group think attitude that all professors were using their graduate students to do research for them and, therefore, she was within her rights to do so. Then, she told me to either do my assigned research paper topic or to drop the class. To her surprise, I dropped the class, and she continued to think that she knew more about morality than God.

8. Evil as Monetary Success

"I think it's a heartless government that will let one baby be born owning a big piece of the country … The least a government could do … is to divide things up fairly among the babies." Kurt Vonnegut, God Bless You Mr. Rosewater

Right now, in Satan's world a handful of powerful people direct billions of other people with their decisions. Currently, 500 people own $7.5 trillion. In fact, 2,000 people own more that the remainder of the world's 6 billion population. Mostly, the power found in these people relates to the fortunes made at other people's expense. If you think about it, there is only so much money to go around in the world, and some people have much more money than their fair share, which means that some people have far less money than their fair share. If you look at the evil of income disparity in the world, you can begin to understand how Satan's evil world works. The people who have the money on earth also have the power that it provides, while people without money have no power. The result is that these powerful people of the upper one percent incomes of the world's population control Satan's systems for the other ninety-nine percent of the world's population. This income and power disparity creates huge social problems, which includes billions of poor people in the world lacking the necessities of adequate food and clean drinking water, while billionaires write off the cost of their $20 million yacht as a second home on their taxes. "Grace be unto you and peace from God the Father, and from our Lord Jesus Christ,

Who gave himself for our sins, that he might deliver us from this present evil world, according to the will of God our Father" (Galatians 1:3-4).

Satan has these one-percenters in charge of maintaining his unfair social, economic, and political systems, and some of these people in charge of Satan's systems do not even know that they are working for Satan as Bellwether people on earth. Many of these upper income one percent Bellwether people don't even consider their vast wealth as evil and somehow believe that they are entitled to it. "God resisteth the proud, but giveth grace unto the humble" (James 4:6). This sense of entitlement to all of this wealth stems from the fact that most members in these Bellwether families have not worked for generations because their wealth just keeps perpetuating itself without any Bellwether family member lifting a finger, while a large percentage of the world's population works to eke out a living by earning $2.00 a day. Therefore, the current living members of a Bellwether family do not know what it means to work or how hard other people work to make a living. "… that if any would not work, neither should he eat" (2 Thessalonians 3:10). In addition, the Bellwether families graze in the upper pastures of society where they will seldom meet with ordinary, hard-working people. If you think about it, Satan's internet world has produced only a handful of people who tell the remainder of the world's population what to do, what to wear, and what to think. Satan rings his Bellwether bell and billions of unthinking people hear it and follow, all the while making the evil systems stronger and the Bellwether families richer. "Love not the world, neither the things that are in the world. If any man love the world, the love of the Father is not in him…. For all that is in the world … is not of the Father…" (1 John 2:15-16).

Unfortunately, many people pursue the dream of someday becoming a Bellwether person themselves, but, in truth, Satan stacks the deck against them. The result is that they spend their entire lives working themselves to death chasing money. At best, making it into the rich Bellwether status is a longshot because the world's systems are rigged by Satan. Yet, despite the long odds, Bellwether seekers continue to press on towards their quest for wealth because Satan knows who he can fool. Both the Bellwether seekers, as well as the Bellwether family members, fit snuggly into Satan's back pocket by correctly filling out Satan's questionnaire for being greedy people. However, many

Bellwether seekers still believe that they can win the evil sweepstakes despite it being mostly a losing battle. Sometimes, however, if they are ambitious, ruthless, and evil enough, Satan just might let them win the Bellwether Prize, which ensures that the world will remain evil and that their souls will go to hell.

However, the Bellwether families already in power aren't very enthusiastic about letting new members into the Bellwether Club. Mostly, their estate gates are closed to the idea. Instead, they prefer that it remain a private club so that they can isolate themselves and their wealth from the rest of the world. And besides, more Bellwether members would further dilute the ranks of their aristocracy in the Bellwether Kingdom. The Bellwether Kingdom already has enough Princes of Industry and Queens of Celebrity. Yet, many an enterprising young Bellwether seeker has climbed close to the top of the Bellwether Mountain only to misstep and have his hopes dashed by Satan. You see, unless the ambitious Bellwether seeker gets a personal RSVP invitation to succeed from Satan who controls the evil systems of the world, he might as well throw down his shovel and pick up his bucket of evil intentions and go home. Thus, Satan's evil physical world will give you a false reading about who you are, about what's important, and about where you're going; while God, Jesus, and the Holy Spirit will work only to increase the spirit of goodness and holiness in you. "And we know that all things work together for good to them that love God, to them who are the called according to his purpose" (Romans 8:28).

9.   Evil as Worshipping Possessions

"The world around us conforms to expectations we place on it."   J. Benson, Haiku to Live By

One afternoon in October on a very sunny day, I was driving home from a college class and encountered a man standing in the street outside a bar bashing his new blue Ford pickup truck with a sledgehammer. The incident happened in the poorest section of town, and the man wielding the sledgehammer looked like he had seen better days. Obviously, the man had been drinking in the bar and had just left the bar, whereupon he found that his new pickup truck would not start. To teach his truck a lesson, he decided to hurt it with a sledgehammer, which was a ridiculous and childish notion, yet he continued to wail on his new pickup truck anyway, producing gashes, creases, and dents all over the truck's body. A few days later, I told this story to a group of people who didn't believe it. Fortunately, a local city bus driver who was at the party had been driving by at the same time as the man was bashing his truck with a sledgehammer and confirmed my story. Over the years, I can still remember the menacing look on the man's face as he destroyed the only new vehicle that he probably had ever owned. His disillusionment over the path of his life must have been very deep for him to calculate that even a shiny new truck had no place in it.

James 4:4 makes it clear where we should place our life's allegiance. "… whosoever therefore will be a friend of the world is the enemy of God." When we rely on the material things of the world to give us self-worth, we have misplaced our spiritual allegiance, for the material things of the world do not interest God and will not give us comfort. And because the material things of the world prove to be a bad judgement on what's important in life, they should not only be meaningless to God but to us as well. Instead of worshipping worldly possessions that will eventually rust, rip, or decay, we should instead be worshipping God. "Lay not up yourselves treasures upon earth, where moth and dust doth corrupt, and where thieves break through and steal; But lay up for yourselves treasures in heaven…" (Matthew 19-20). Although Satan has made worldly things very convenient and attractive for us to worship to distract us from our real importance in the world to worship God, we should not buy into it. "Submit yourselves therefore to God. Resist the devil and he will flee from you" (James 4:7).

Therefore, the more you resist worshiping material things provided in this world by Satan to establish your self-worth, the more you will come to understand what's really important in your life, and you will begin to devote more of your time to the sacred worship of Jesus who is speaking to you through the Holy Spirit to guide you to your spiritual self. So, what you decide to worship is both an individual time and a personal inclination issue. The more time that you spend worshipping God, the less time you spend worshipping the corrupt world and Satan's things in it, and the greater the inclination will become to worship God and to learn more about living in your Spirit by reading the Bible. Jesus said, "I pray for them: I pray not for the world, but for them which thou hast given me; for they are thine" (John 17:9). This equation, however, is lost on most people because their lives are consumed by pursuing the worldliness of material possessions and power in a flawed world as provided by Satan, and the time left to worship God, read the Bible, and live in the Spirit often becomes an after-thought or no thought at all. "For what is a man profited, if he shall gain the whole world, and lose his soul?" (Matthew 16:26)

The number of breaths that you take in a day is the exact number of breaths that God gives to you. You cannot by yourself get one more breath of life from the world than the number of breaths allotted to you by God. Therefore, if you don't worship God who gave you the breath of life in the first place, it is being disrespectful to God your Creator and His Son Jesus Christ. So, the question becomes: If you ignore God long enough by not praying to thank Him for your existence and for giving you the breath of life in the first place, will He, in turn, begin to ignore you? The answer to that question is a curious one. Because of God's infinite grace, His forgiving nature, and His pending gift of salvation through Jesus Christ, He will never forget about you while you're in Satan's grasp. In fact, because of God's endless supply of forgiving grace, every soul still has a chance to get to heaven through His Son Jesus Christ. "I am the way, the truth, and the life: no man cometh unto the Father, but by me" (John 14:6). Yet why would anyone continue to put their faith and value in the false hope of the things found in Satan's world, when they could be praying for Jesus' forgiveness right now?

"Cardiac Christian" is often a term reserved for those people who call upon the name of the Lord on their deathbed after a severe heart attack while living a secular life. I submit that their heart problems started long before their heart attacked them physically; their heart problems started spiritually when they accepted the world of Satan and ignored God and the Lord Jesus by not taking them into their heart by listening to the Holy Spirit.

The poet WD Snodgrass once wrote a poem after his own heart attack. The poem's title was "The Day My Heart Attacked." The poem's title makes the point that your heart can physically turn on you from the inside and attack you without warning. A physical part of you that you had trusted and depended upon all your life has suddenly turned against you. Beyond physically attacking and failing you, your heart can also fail you spiritually by not listening to the Holy Spirit within you to heal your own soul. If your heart can attack you physically, then it can also attack your spiritually. After all, if your heart listens to Satan's worldly deceptions long enough, over time you will simply die spiritually and succumb to the Evil One. Overall, it becomes a choice of which entity you want to worship. Will you give what time God has created for you on earth to worship the physical worldliness of Satan by sledgehammering your way through life? Or will you reject Satan and give your attention to God, who gave you your life and its time on earth in the first place? "For where your treasure is, there will your heart be also" (Matthew 6:21). The choice is yours, and the clock is ticking.

10. Evil Money with Good Intentions

"It didn't occur to me until later that there's another truth ... greed in a good cause is still greed." Stephen King, Wolves of the Calla

So, what's the point to all this talk about "think for yourself" in Satan's mass-produced evil world and don't follow the ring of Satan's bell in a Bellwether world of immorality? Well, it's about Satan's control of the world's economic, political, and social systems, and its influence on your life. Until Christ's returns to earth in triumph, Satan will temporarily control how the world functions. Ever wonder why there is so much injustice and corruption in the world? The reason for this chaotic mess is because Satan is in charge of it. Why is there war, poverty, and injustice? It is Satan's goal to use money, power, and greed to move as many people into thoughtless action as possible and closer towards the cliffs of hell. Once Satan can get them to stand at the brink of hell, then from there it's just a gentle push over the edge. "In whom the god of this world hath blinded the minds of them which believe not.... (2 Corinthians 4:4).

Years ago, I was courted by a television station to work for it in the sales department. The sales manager for the television station was convinced that I was the man for the job, but the television station's owner wasn't convinced about hiring me. This resulted in a two-month long stand-off between the owner and the sales manager over whether to hire me. In the meantime, I had taken a job at a department store selling furniture; it was just after I had been honorably discharged from the US Army, and at the time I really didn't know what I wanted to do with my life. I had been working in the furniture store for about a month when the sales manager from the television station showed up one day to inform me that he had convinced the television station's owner to hire me. The television station's job paid twice the money as the work at the furniture store, yet I had already committed to the employment at the furniture store. When I told the television station sales manager that I couldn't leave the furniture store because they had hired me and were training me, the television station sales manager couldn't believe his ears. He was convinced that the higher wage at the television station and my own greed would certainly leverage me away from working at the department store. When I told him that I had a job, he responded that my work selling furniture wasn't a job but a waste of time. I told him that he had waited too long to hire me and that in the interim I had found other employment. Granted, the furniture store job wasn't the greatest work in the world, but the store had been kind enough to hire a recently discharged veteran who didn't know what he wanted to do with his life, and I had to honor their commitment to me. My friends also could not believe my decision to stay at the department store because they had been convinced by Satan that money was the only influencer in the world. I told them that money shouldn't drive a decision but honor and commitment to one's word. "Whoso keepeth the commandment shall feel no evil thing: and a wise man's heart discerneth both time and judgement" (Ecclesiastes 8:5).

To nudge people to the brink of hell, Satan always uses money to influence their behavior. Money creates violent reactions in people, and Satan almost always uses money to promote evil in some way. Even when money is used for a seemingly good purpose, if you look deeper and behind the façade, you'll usually find a corrupt intention by someone. Simply put, money corrupts the soul and Satan knows and uses it for outward or inward evil purposes. If man cannot resist the greed in his heart put there by Satan, then evil will take up residence there. Therefore, why people give money and why people accept it is a heart issue because the exchange of money reveals something about the degree of pureness in the soul concerning the transaction. Satan will always be the primary banker in the world, and he will always use money as a primary conduit to make sure that money is used for evil purposes. His intent is to make people worship it, and tempers will flare when he succeeds. Whenever there is a contention about money, people always see red.

It's true that Satan's evil and greedy influence in the world has hot-wired people to go ballistic over money disputes. Going emotionally ballistic about money seems to be part of Satan's landscape for corruption. For example, former loving family siblings get into fierce legal arguments over the equal dividing of the estate of a recently deceased parent. Employers continually fight with employees over fair wages. Buying possessions is always used by Satan as an enchantment, yet everything costs too much. When possessions are owned by others, it creates envy, jealousy, and strife. "Be not envious against evil men, neither desire to be with them" (Proverbs 24:1). In Satan's world, our paycheck will never be large enough because Satan uses money to bring out the worst in human behavior. The irony, of course, is that while greedy people strive for more money and are never content, all the while Satan is sowing evil in their heart as they seek to define themselves by what they own. Ironically, when their unholy ambitions and greed are rewarded by a pay raise, they believe that they are winning in the game of life, when they are unfortunately losing their soul. Once again, Satan has turned the tables on them because all the while their evil action motivated by money is hurting their Spirit and leading them down a path to hell where someday they will have to make a final payment.

Because Satan controls the systems on earth, he will make sure that hell is never full. He will never hang out a "No Vacancy" sign in hell because he will always be at work ruining lives and building additions in hell to make sure there is adequate room. "Hell and destruction are never full; so the eyes of man are never satisfied" (Proverbs 27:20) Ironically, all the while Satan is busy constructing new additions in hell to accommodate the sinful overflow of corrupt and greedy people, the future greedy residents of hell are smugly thinking about how smart they are on earth for outwitting others while whistling a happy tune in Satan's key. For many people, it is easier for them to follow Satan in the here-and-now and to forget about the eternal consequences for their soul. For now, they might think that It is easier for them to take credit for the work done by a co-worker rather than for them to do the work themselves. Yet, with each tick of the clock the day of reckoning approaches for their eternal destination. "Fight the good fight of faith, lay hold on eternal life, whereunto thou art also called..." (1 Timothy 6:12).

11. Evil as Normal

"The greatest temptations are not those that solicit our consent to obvious sin, but those that offer us great evils masking as the greatest goods." Thomas Merton, No Man is an Island

Many years ago, while a student in college I received a letter of recommendation from a professor. I have always remembered this letter of recommendation because it contained a curious observation in it about me. In the letter of recommendation, a sentence stated: "He is a rare person because he is a man who thinks for himself." At the time, I thought everyone thought for themselves. For instance, every day we make decisions, yet over the years I have begun to understand my mentor's meaning. It's true that we make decisions for ourselves every day, but the point to this sentence is not focused on the everyday decision; it is focused only on the moral decisions that we make and the implications of those decisions. In short, do we have the courage to make decisions solely on moral principle when the Holy Spirit speaks to us, or do we acquiesce to the convenience of Satan's immoral moment? When a weighty decision of moral consequence presents itself, do we stand firm with the Lord or do we take the easy way out and succumb to the temptations of Satan?

Revelation Chapter 13:3 states, "… and all the world wondered after the beast." The beast, of course, is Satan. To "wonder" after something means to release your sense of logic and its application to a problem. To wonder means to be awed by something and to be so struck by it that the wonder releases you from your normal thinking process. In short, you are so emotionally dumbfounded that you can't think straight. This is the case with people today who can't think straight to fight the Beast to get passed the temptations of Satan. The Beast has many people dumbfounded by his magic and the power of evil over them. Make no mistake about Satan's presence: It is not the possession (e.g., boat, car, house, job, or power) that has the hold over you. It is Satan's power behind the possession. By worshipping money, possessions, greed, and power, people are not really worshipping the object; they are worshipping Satan's evil intent that resides behind it.

"And all that dwell upon the earth shall worship him…" (Revelation 13:8). That's right, the earth is Satan's domain for the time being until the Lord Jesus returns. So, for now, we live in a world steeped in Satan's evil influence, and only those people who can think morally and

Biblically for themselves can fight the pervasive temptations of the beast of hell. And those people who have the courage to resist Satan's temptations by wearing the moral cloak of Jesus Christ are written as an entry in the Book of Life. The Book of Life lists the names of all God's people who have come to His son Jesus Christ for the gift of salvation. Jesus has known these people—His own, and these people can resist Satan's temptations to walk an upright path in life by making Christian-based, moral decisions as stated in the Bible's scripture. "Then said Jesus to them again, Peace be unto you: as my Father hath sent me, even so send I you. And when he had said this, he breathed on them, and saith unto them, Receive ye the Holy Ghost" (John 20:21-22). Therefore, people who have not received Christ as their savior are probably worshipping Satan in some worldly behavior. It sounds harsh, but it is true. "And all that dwell upon the earth shall worship him (Satan), whose names are not written in the book of life of the Lamb (Jesus) slain from the foundation of the world" (Revelation 13:8).

Therefore, Jesus died for you and for your sins so that you could have a chance at redeeming your soul. Rather than worshiping the temporary trinkets of Satan, you now have the option of worshipping Jesus Christ, living in the Spirit, and getting your soul saved for eternity. But you must think for yourself and fight the beast of hell to help Jesus in the redemption of your soul by turning away from the "normal" secular influences of Satan and turning towards the saving grace offered by Jesus Christ, and this requires reading the Bible and the courage to turn your back on the world and on Satan's devices that seek to entice you. Everyone will tell you to accept the normal beastly ways of the physical world, and you must defy that advice and Satan by deciding to travel morally in your spiritual self by following your heart and the Bible. If you listen to your Holy Spirit and the supernatural communication of Jesus in your heart and read His Word in the Bible, then you can wrestle with the devil with the supernatural strength of God's eternal plan for you.

12. Evil as Bad Luck

"People shouldn't call for demons unless they really mean what they say." CS Lewis, The Last Battle

When I was younger man and before I accepted Jesus Christ as my personal savior, Satan made everything in my life difficult. Back then,

The Beast was a relentless force, and he loved to set traps for me to discourage me from seeking Jesus. Whether the event in my life was large or small, it didn't matter; Satan was always there to disrupt my life. I'll give you an example of what I mean; it was a small and meaningless incident, but at the time Satan inflated it into a big deal.

One winter morning while I was walking to my car from my apartment, I saw a large man in a long burgundy coat walking one hundred feet in front of me. The snowfall was heavy that winter, and a three feet crust of old snow had been joined the previous night by four inches of new snow, which made the sidewalk and parking lot slippery. As it turned out, the man's car was parked next to mine, and I reduced the cadence of my walk to give him enough time to get into his car. So, while I waited for him to get into his car, I saw him reach for his car's door handle, slip on the ice in the parking lot, and fall backwards against my car. When I reached my car in the parking lot, he had already stood upright and was dusting the snow off his long coat. I asked him if he was all right, and it was then that I noticed that his fall backwards had created a big dent in my right front fender. The dent was about the size of a basketball, so I said, "You fell on my car and dented the fender," to which he replied, "No I didn't," and hurriedly got into his car and drove away, never to be seen again. "He that covereth his sins shall not prosper: but whoso confesseth and forsaketh them shall have mercy" (Proverbs 28:13)."

At the time, I was driving a rusted out old beater of a Pontiac. It was a junk heap to be sure, but nonetheless, there was now a new dent in the fender, and I was determined to get satisfaction for it. Despite my car being in a ruinous condition, Satan had convinced me that I needed to be repaid for the damage done to it. Satan had forgotten to remind me that the floor of my car was so rusted out that I could see the road beneath the car and that at any moment I expected to fall through the floor and be run over by my own car. So, a few days later, I showed up at my insurance agent's office to file a claim, yet when I told him what had happened, he just laughed and told me that I couldn't file a claim under the circumstances. To which, I replied, "Why not? It's just a simple case of hit and run." Isn't it just like Satan to turn things around—make a person hit your car instead of the car hitting a person.

During that entire year, my unfortunate circumstances never ended:

Cars wouldn't start, checks got lost in the mail, money stolen, and apartments burglarized. One afternoon I returned home from the grocery store to find a man carrying my little black-and-white television set with the rabbit ears out my bedroom window. I caught him straddling the windowsill, just as he was half-way out the window. "Why are you stealing my little worthless back and white tv set," I screamed. "Go out to the suburbs and steal a large color one." The burglar must have taken my advice to heart, for he suddenly dropped my tv and it smashed on the floor before he made his escape

Of course, Satan enjoyed my misery that year. Every day he took sandpaper to my skin to watch me bleed, and he enjoyed watching me wince in my discomfort. I bet those souls in hell heard my screams; that is, until one day in the depths of my deepest despair, I heard the Holy Spirit's voice speak to me. A small quiet space in my heart whispered, "This is only Satan's strategy to prevent you from listening to me. His world is full of distractive noises and quick fixes. Yet here I am within you; a holy and quiet place where Jesus awaits." Years later, I understood that if Satan can prevent you from listening to your Holy Spirit long enough by making you suffer, then maybe you will forget about doing any soul-searching. Because once you start seeking your spiritual self by listening to your Holy Spirit, praying to Jesus, and reading the Bible, Satan knows that you are now employing the best spiritual weapons of self-defense against him. With prayer, you are now protecting yourself against his supernatural evil by using the full spiritual armor of God. "And he (Jesus) spake a parable unto them to this end, that men ought always to pray, and not to faint;" (Luke 18:1). So, Satan's goal is to keep you from hearing the spiritual truth that God awaits in you to guide you on a holy path. Satan wants you to believe that living in the perpetual evil in the world is your only option.

Yet, because Jesus has imparted the Holy Spirit as a spiritual Comforter, there is another body living inside of you that is not subject to being held captive by the physical bonds of Satan. You don't have to live like Satan wants you to. You don't have to be his slave to sin on earth. You don't have to live solely in the physical confines of his domain because you also have a spiritual body that can soar above and beyond all earthly trouble. "Henceforth, let no man trouble me, for I bear in my body the marks of the Lord Jesus" (Galatians 6:17). Satan, of course, won't tell you that Jesus has given you an escape route from his fallen world; Satan is only interested in handing you another beer. But your spiritual body lives outside of Satan's physical realm, and it's a celestial place where you can find personal peace amid the world's chaos and corruption. When you live in the Spirit of Jesus' gift of salvation, no harm can come to you in this world because you have been assured a place with Jesus in heaven, but to experience this personal peace you must live in the Spirit and not in the flesh. "Examine yourselves, whether ye be in the faith; prove your own selves. Know ye not your own selves, how that Jesus Christ is in you …" (2 Corinthians 13:5).

CHAPTER TWO

REASONS TO LIVE IN THE SPIRIT

"Except a man be born of water and of the spirit, he cannot enter into the Kingdom of God." —John 3:5

1. To Understand Life Before It is too Late

Many years ago, I was teaching at a small liberal arts college in Iowa. The college had a diverse international student population, and the student body was comprised of students from fourteen countries. One year, as the end of the academic year approached, I was asked by three Ugandan students to spend the summer in Uganda with them. They all lived on the shores of Lake Victoria, which is the second largest freshwater lake in the world. As they explained, Lake Victoria had miles of sand beach, and I could write in the morning in a small guest cottage near the lake, and in the afternoon we could all go to the beach, spread our blankets, and take a nap. As the students further explained, it was all right to take a nap on the sand beach because the crocodiles hardly ever came up to shore. Hardly ever, of course, meant that sometimes they did. Can you imagine sleeping on the beach in the warm sun where the annual mean temperature in mid-June is 72 degrees and waking up with a huge crocodile standing over you? Or, worse yet, waking up with one of your arms missing. The point is that what you can't see or what you choose to ignore can sometimes come back to bite you.

2. To Understand Life's Purpose

"This getting born business is not as simple as it seemed...." Robert Penn Warren, The Whole Question

In Matthew 10:28, Jesus tells us "... fear not them which kill the body, but are not able to kill the soul: but rather fear him (i.e., Satan) which is able to destroy both body and soul in hell." Therefore, there are men who can kill your body, but if you are right with God, Jesus, and Holy Spirit, then these men cannot really hurt you because your soul will be going to heaven to be with Jesus. Your physical body is secondary to your spiritual body. Your physical body is merely the vessel that contains your spirit/soul on earth. It's true, however, that because your body contains your soul, when you hurt the physical body you also hurt the spiritual body. Yet, the physical body is only the container for the spiritual body.

For instance, if you drop a can off a kitchen shelf and it crashes to the floor, the container becomes dented and it damages the contents inside because the contents are now disturbed and not in their original condition. In the same way, because the physical body contains the soul when you hurt the physical body by abusing it like with drugs, alcohol, and unchristian behavior you also hurt or injure the soul inside as well. At a grocery store, people will avoid buying a dented can on the shelf. It is perceived as a flaw that has damaged the can's contents. Sometimes, even when you really need the contents of the can, you still won't buy it in a damaged container. It works the same way with the physical body and the soul. A person who continually damages the physical container of their body will eventually damage their soul inside. Jesus calls your physical body the "Holy Temple" for your soul because it contains the Holy Spirit—God in you. "Know ye not that ye are the temple of God, and that the Spirit of God dwelleth in you? If any man defile the temple of God, him shall God destroy; for the temple of God is holy, which temple ye are" (1 Corinthians 16-17). Thus, every time you excessively indulge in unchristian behavior and in a substance that hurts your physical body, you are also hurting your spiritual body by offending the Holy Spirit, which God has placed inside of you to be your spiritual guide and Comforter. "Howbeit when he, the Spirit of truth, is come, he will guide you in all truth… (John 16:13). When you neglect taking care of your physical body, you also neglect God by not taking care of the Holy Spirit within you.

Years ago, when my two children were in elementary school, we drove around in the family car early on Saturday mornings searching for five-cent deposit aluminum cans to redeem that were discarded along the highway. It was a source of money for my children to buy miscellaneous items like candy. So, every Saturday morning after breakfast, my son, daughter, and I would load-in one large trash bag into the car's backseat and drive down a five-mile stretch of rural road looking for aluminum cans. While my children hung their heads out the car windows spotting cans, I drove at five miles per hour listening to the car radio. When they spotted a can, I'd pull my car over to the side of the road, get out, and retrieve the can from the ditch. However, sometimes when they spotted a can and I went to retrieve it, it turned out not to be a can with a five-cent deposit stamp on it so I'd throw it back unto the ground.

One Saturday morning, I was in the process of turning the car around to head for home when my son spotted one last can in the ditch. It's true that we had already collected our limit of twenty cans (i.e., $1.00), but with one last can just setting there, I pulled over to the side of the road, stopped the car, and walked down into the ditch to retrieve it. When I picked up the can, I noticed that it didn't have a five-cent deposit stamp on it, so I threw it back onto the ground. Unfortunately, just as the can left my hand to throw it down onto the ground, an Iowa State Police car drove over a small hill and a State Trooper saw the can leaving my hand. Suddenly, the Iowa State Police car screeched to a halt next to my parked car, and the Iowa State Trooper jumped out of his car and ran over to me, whereupon he accused me of being a litterbug, which carried a $500 fine. He had only seen the can leaving my hand; he had not seen me pick up the can to look at it. Thus, I was accused of being a litterbug, although by driving my children around to pick up cans along the roadside, I was actually doing the opposite—picking up other people's discarded trash.

I could tell by the Sate Trooper's flushed face that he was in no mood for a litterbug this early on a Saturday morning, so I had to defend my actions quickly. I pointed to my kids in the car, explained that every Saturday morning that we filled a trash bag with discarded aluminum cans found along the roadside but that we only kept the cans with a five-cent deposit. The State Trooper looked towards my car, whereupon my son held up the trash bag of cans as evidence to support my case. The State Police Trooper then looked at the ground and apologized. He had only seen me throwing away the can, although now he realized that there was more to the story.

And that's how easy things in life can appear to be one thing but, in truth, are another. And that's the way life operates. On one hand, Satan's world seems to be filled with irresistible shiny objects like that last aluminum can alongside the roadside, but upon closer examination, the shiny objects are worthless, although we often spend a lifetime searching for them. However, if by living in the Spirit you can see the real value of what's important in life, then you can discard Satan's worthless objects and have a chance to evaluate your life by living from the perspective of the Spirit. Seeing life through the Spirit's Eyes of

Understanding gives you an entirely new truth-filled perspective about yourself and about the world, one that doesn't throw away your life by pursuing worthless things, but one that focuses on Jesus and His gift of salvation for you.

Therefore, you are really two people—not one. You are not only a physical person, but you are also a spiritual person; the two of you co-exist. And when you damage one, you also damage the other. That is why people read the Bible. It not only feeds the body's intellect (i.e., the brain), but it also feeds the soul (i.e., heart). By understanding God's Word in your mind (body), and then holding it in your heart (soul), you become a well-balanced and more holy and spiritual person. "What? know ye not that your body is the temple of the Holy Ghost, which is in you, which ye have of God, and ye are not your own" (Corinthians 6:19). Neglecting God's Word in the Bible to know more about Jesus and to build a spiritual relationship with Him will not feed either your body (intellect) or your soul (spirit). In fact, many people today are starving their soul by not reading the Bible. God's Word in the Bible is the nutritional source for your soul. It provides you with the power of proper moral health to guide you to good behavior that feeds your spirit, which leads to both good intellectual and spiritual health in life. God's Word in the Bible will not only go to your head, but it will also go to your heart.

3. To Fill Life's Void and Disappointments

"Like so many Americans, she was trying to construct a life that made sense from things she found in gift shops." Kurt Vonnegut, Slaughterhouse Five

Years ago, I knew a man who was the son of a missionary stationed in Africa. For the first fifteen years of this man's life, he had lived in the remote jungle far away from civilization. Instead of playing baseball, he threw stones at crocodiles in a nearby river. When his father decided to bring his family back to the United States, he brought them back in a unique way—on a freighter. There were only 12 other passengers on the freighter, along with the cargo of African goods. It would take the freighter three weeks to sail from Africa to New York, and my friend had no idea of how to spend the time. He read books in his cabin for the first few days, and then he saw her, a beautiful young girl his age—the daughter of a diplomat on the freighter's deck. He was instantly in love.

Admittedly, he was somewhat socially awkward. Growing up your first fifteen years of life in the remote regions of the African jungle will do that to a guy. Yet, he was determined to overcome his social awkwardness and his fright and introduce himself to her. When he had the occasion to introduce himself, he had accidently met her on the deck of the ship, which he had only been on once for a brief time, so he had not really experienced firsthand the rolling 20-foot swells of the North Atlantic Ocean. And it did not take him long to understand that he was immediately seasick. For some reason, his seasickness had not affected him when he was below deck in his cabin, yet while here on deck next to the rail he suddenly turned green and vomited, just as the young lady approached him. Despite overcoming his awkwardness and enjoying the advantage he had as the only other teenager on board, he could not meet with the girl on deck without getting sick. The cabins below deck were without air-conditioning, so everyone on board congregated every day on deck to socialize and to feel the soft summer breeze, except him who had to stay below in the cabin's void and the intense heat for the entire three weeks.

Therefore, even when we have home-court advantage, we can still be blind-sided by some other dilemma that we cannot foresee. This is how Satan's world works; just when you think that you have it made, Satan turns the tables on you and something else happens to create a void. The tribulations in Satan's world are many and can strike without warning, but the choice is still yours to follow your physical self or to follow your spiritual self. "Wherefore laying aside all malice, and all guile, and hypocrisies, and envies, and all evil speakings, As newborn babes, desire the sincere milk of the word, that ye may grow thereby" (1Peter: 1-2). You can't do both; you must choose one way to live or the other. Granted, it might take some time to discern the Holy Spirit's voice in you and to get used to living in your spiritual self because we are fallen creatures living in Satan's control of the physical world, and it might take some time for you to learn and adopt a Christian lifestyle that applies Jesus' principles of morality by reading the Bible. "But God hath chosen the foolish things of the world to confound the wise; and God hath chosen the weak things of the world to confound the things which are mighty" (1 Corinthians1:27). But it is never too late to forsake the appeal of Satan's physical world and to crossover to live in the Spirit with a Christian's perspective. And young or old, this is what

God wants and expects of you: First, He wants you to listen and to follow the moral center found in your Holy Spirit and He expects you to heed the voice of the Holy Spirit, the spiritual entity that Jesus has sent to you as a spiritual guide and Comforter while you live in Satan's fallen world. Second, God expects you to pray to Jesus Christ for guidance and for forgiveness to cast away your former sinful self so that you can make progress towards salvation. Third, God expects you to read the Bible for moral instruction to strengthen your spiritual self to defend yourself against Satan and to know and understand Jesus' role in securing and saving our soul for eternity. Fourth, He expects you to start attending church to be with other more experienced Christian people who began learning about God, Jesus, and the Holy Spirit years ago and who started in the same place where you are now in growing your Christian holy self. "I am the vine, ye are the branches: He that abideth in me, and I in him, the same bringeth forth much fruit: for without me ye can do nothing" (John 15:5).

John 14:23-27 makes it clear that we are not only physical beings but spiritual beings as well. No one should doubt this fact, especially not after Jesus says specifically that God and Jesus will live in us if we follow God's Word. "If a man love me, he will keep my words: and my Father will love him, and we will come unto him, and make our abode with him" (John 14:23). So, no matter how lonely Satan might make you feel in the shell of your physical body, you are never alone because the Spirit of God lives in you. Your job is to find God's spiritual indwelling in you by loving Jesus and by reading and keeping His Word. Therefore, you are not physically alone on earth making choices by yourself, as Satan would like you to believe. But you have also been spiritually befriended by God, who lives in you. To receive and maintain God's spiritual grace, you need to love Jesus and live your life according to His instruction in the Bible. If you do these two things—love Jesus and follow His Word—then God will also love you and will reside with you through the Holy Spirit. "Let us hear the conclusion of the whole matter: Fear God, and keep his commandments: for this is the whole duty of man" (Ecclesiastes 12:13).

Although many people deny the existence of their spiritual self by following Satan in the physical world and ignoring God's Word by blocking out the Holy Spirit's interior voice speaking to them, they do so at their own peril. "Now therefore fear the Lord, and serve him in sincerity and in truth: and put away the gods which your fathers served on the other side of the flood, and in Egypt; and serve ye the Lord" (Joshua 24:14). There is more to life than the physical world. People often both deny or ignore God's spirit living in them and don't listen to their inner voice and don't want to follow God's rules for living a moral life. They want to do things their way. Perhaps, they are also afraid to follow God's Word and to hold up their own lifestyle to His light because it would be apparent that they are living a sinful life. "Repent ye therefore, and be converted, that your sins may be blotted out, when the times of refreshing shall come from the presence of the Lord" (Acts 4:19). Unfortunately, those people who turn their back on Jesus (The Son) and God (The Father) by not listening to the inner voice (the Holy Spirit) and by not praying and following the Bible's commandments will suffer and live in the void of the consequences. "The man that wandereth out of the way of understanding shall remain in the congregation of the dead" (Proverbs 21:16). Therefore, it is not only Jesus's voice in you telling you to love and to follow His instructions for your spiritual well-being, but it is also the voice of God, the Father, and the Creator of the Universe! And then, as if being called spiritually by a voice from Jesus and God isn't enough, they will also send you a teacher—the Holy Spirit—inside of you that will continue to guide and comfort you in your physical state while you become more spiritually holy through following God's Word.

So, a larger question becomes: "Why doesn't Jesus in His infinite supernatural power simply wave His hand to make everyone automatically hear the voice of the Holy Spirit calling to them in their heart?" The answer is that approaching God is a two-way street. It would be easy and certainly within God's infinite power to embed the Holy Spirit's voice into everyone's mind and heart. Yet, God wants our participation in the process. We—by God—are given a choice to hear His Word in our heart, as spoken by the Holy Spirit—or not. If we want to turn our back on Jesus, He allows it because He has given us our own "free will" to listen to Him or not.

Satan provides many distractions in the physical world, and Satan's role is to denounce Jesus and to convince you that there is nothing more to find after you have experienced the lusts of the physical world. Satan says that this world, which he temporarily controls until Christ's return—is all there is, so you better take what you can get in the physical world because nothing exists beyond it. The Bible references these people in 2 Peter 2:12. "But these, as natural beasts, made to be taken and destroyed, speak evil things that they understand not; and shall utterly perish in their own corruption." Therefore, because some people have chosen through their own free will to turn their back on the Holy Trinity, they will never understand the true story of their life – that Satan's way only provides voids and disappointments. If they had chosen to follow Jesus instead of Satan to know and to follow the holy teachings of Jesus Christ as revealed to them through their own internal Holy Spirit and the Bible, then they would have come to recognize their own holiness within themselves. Instead, they chose to follow the external path of Satan and by their own choice and ignorance "… shall receive the reward of unrighteousness, as they that count it pleasure to riot in the day time…" (2 Peter 2:13).

Therefore, while God has the power to bestow His holy righteousness on everyone, He gives humankind a participating role in becoming a righteous follower of God. Without people seeking God, God will not simply give people His righteousness. They need to seek God because God is God, and they have to come to the realization that they need God, Jesus, and the Holy Spirit in their life. Without that spiritual connection and that acknowledgement, people will continue to flail about in life in disappointment because of their own human frailty. "Trust in the Lord with all thine might; and lean not unto thine own understanding (Proverbs 3:5).

No doubt, we will have a difficult time as spiritual beings during Satan's temporary reign on earth, and we are invited by God in John 14:23-27 to recognize our spiritual essence to fill the void and disappointment by listening to the Holy Spirit's voice within us, and we receive three invitations: one from Jesus, one from God, and one from the Holy Spirit to do so. Three invitations have been sent to you by the voices of the Holy Trinity to recognize that God dwells in you as a Spirit. You have been given three invitations to recognize God's spiritual body within you, and these three holy invitations should not be ignored. It is time to pray and fill the void and disappointment in life. God, Jesus, and the Holy Spirit—The Holy Trinity—is awaiting your RSVP.

4. To Establish Moral and Social Compass

"Moderation in all things, especially moderation" —Ralph Waldo Emerson, The Conduct of Life

Many years ago, my wife and I were dining at an exclusive French restaurant. It was May, and the early spring freshness of flowers and green grass were in the air. And so apparently was romance. Unfortunately, on the night that my wife and I had chosen to dine out was also prom night, and hundreds of high schoolers were dining out as well prior to the prom dance. For a while at the restaurant, it was fun to watch the colorful dresses of the young women and to watch the behavior of the young men as they tried to navigate through the political positions of prom night. For the most part, it took me back to my own prom days when social and dinner etiquette were still somewhat foreign to me. Yet, not far into our meal, my wife and I witnessed something so out of proportion with the formal style of the evening that it still resonates today in our casual conversations with others. Halfway through my dessert of poached pear with cracked pepper, a young prom-goer arrived with his date. He was wearing the required tuxedo, and his date was dressed in a striking purple prom dress. Yet, curiously, he was also carrying a Campbell's tomato soup can in his right hand, which he proudly set down on the table in front of his chair. I nodded at my wife, and we both took note of the can on the table. Then, it happened, just after he had properly seated his date by pulling out her chair – and before he was seated himself—he picked up the Campbell's soup can and spit a huge wad of tobacco juice into it. As the tobacco juice dripped from his chin, he politely sat down across the table from his date, who didn't seem to mind the tobacco juice sliding down his chin. Somehow, his repugnant behavior at the highest social event of the year had not bothered her, although it immensely disturbed many other diners by the grimacing looks on their faces. Then, she reached into her dainty prom-night purse and pulled out her own Campbell's tomato soup can: set it down proudly in front of her on the dinner table, took a great quid of tobacco between her thumb and forefinger from a tobacco pouch in her purse, stuck the quid of tobacco into her mouth, and eased it with her tongue into a big ball on the inside of her right cheek. By this time, some restaurant patrons had had enough and decided to call it quits on prom night dinner, and they stood up and left the restaurant.

Over the years when I have related this story to others, I have also asked myself many questions about this restaurant incident. The main question always circles back to: Did they chew tobacco on prom night because it was an outrageous act that would disgust others? Or did they chew tobacco at the dinner table on prom night because they chewed tobacco at the dinner table every night? I will never know the answer to this question, yet it is at the heart of the incident. The first possibility—that they did it to socially outrage others—makes it somehow an interesting statement about the superficial nature of prom night. However, if they were habitual tobacco chewers at dinner—then it made their behavior more inappropriate and disgusting.

In Satan's world, it is difficult to know what motivates people's behavior. In fact, inappropriate and immoral behavior takes place so often that it has almost become commonplace. Usually, Satan likes to offer up immoral behavior with shock value so that the shock value makes the bad behavior seem innocent and fun. Many times, the irreverent actions like the tomato soup can tobacco-chewing couple at prom night dinner are often viewed as funny and go viral on the internet. In Satan's world, dumbing down social sensibilities and politeness makes it easier to control people. Criminal law states that "ignorance of the law is no excuse." That is, if you break criminal law unknowingly, it is still breaking the law and you are still held responsible for your unlawful actions. However, today if you break social or moral laws intentionally, its element of humor often seems to absolve you from any punishment. In today's world, it seems like anything goes, especially if by Satan's standards the behavior is so outrageous that it seems funny. However, there is nothing funny about Satan's influencing your behavior or anyone's reaction to it. "For to be carnally minded is death; but to be spiritually minded is life and peace" (Romans 8:6). Satan doesn't care about your or anyone else's sensibilities; he cares about the control he exerts over you so that he can take you to hell. If he can control your behavior without you questioning it under the disguise of making it look outrageous and funny, then he has the first step to the basket on you for taking your soul to hell. Yet, despite Satan's cruel antics to disguise crude behavior as acceptable, moral and social boundaries do exist in the Bible and for good reason: they maintain social and moral order, although Satan would like you to think that his disorder is normal, and it is—if you follow along and accept his no-moral-boundaries solution to making your decisions in life. 2 Thessalonians 2:12 addresses the problem in not believing in boundaries, "That they all might be damned who believed not the truth, but had pleasure in unrighteousness."

5.   To Avoid Selfishness

"Either you must do something, or something must be done to you." Herman Melville, Bartleby the Scrivener

Years ago, a student of mine wrote an essay about something evil that she did as a 14-year-old girl. Her parents owned an RV, and they wanted her to go on a two-week vacation with them. She didn't want to go; instead, she wanted to stay at home to party with her friends. Unfortunately, her parents insisted that she go with them and she went. On the first day of their vacation, they stopped in the afternoon to eat lunch at a roadside picnic table. According to her, it was a beautiful June afternoon; the sun was beaming in a cloudless blue sky. Thus far, she had been so angry about being made by her parents to go on "their" vacation that she had not spoken one word to them. When they were seated at the picnic table eating lunch, she still refused to speak to her parents. She avoided any eye contact with them and looked down at the top of the picnic table. That's when she saw her father's wallet fall out of his back pocket onto the ground when he stood up to clear the paper plates after lunch. She saw the wallet hit the picnic table's bench seat and then fall under the table. And that's when her plan to get back home to party with her friends began to hatch. So, she didn't tell her father about the wallet that had fallen out of his pocket; he wouldn't discover his missing wallet until 200 miles later when he reached for it in his back pants pocket to pay for gas at a convenience gas station. Then, she watched as her father and mother frantically searched the RV for the wallet, and she remained silent as she heard her parents retraced their steps back to the park where they had stopped to eat lunch. They quickly drove back the 200 miles to where they had stopped to eat lunch that afternoon, and there under the picnic table they found her dad's wallet. By now, her parents were both emotionally drained and relieved to find the wallet; her dad's wallet contained most of the cash and credit cards for their trip. In fact, her parents were so emotionally distraught after losing the wallet and having to backtrack 200 miles towards home to retrieve it that they decided to cancel the entire trip. By now, the sun was starting to set, and with a little luck they could be sleeping in their own beds by sundown.

It's evident from this story that Satan doesn't have age requirements for suggesting evil behavior. He doesn't care how old you are. In fact, he prefers that you start to follow him at an early age. The Bible, of course, has a famous verse concerning the relationship of children to their parents. Most people have heard the verse in Exodus 20:12 "Honor thy father and thy mother." Yet, few people know the remainder of the verse that describes what will happen to your life if you do. "Honor thy father and thy mother: that thy days may be long upon the land which the Lord thy God giveth thee." In short, if you honor thy father and thy mother, God will promise you a long life. However, if Satan can convince you that evil is good at an early age, then he will have an even better chance of convincing you of that when you get older. Therefore, despite the girl seemingly getting her way and getting to go back home from a vacation to party with her friends, she was not the winner of this incident. Satan was the winner, and the sooner in life that people understand that they are living two lives simultaneously—one in the flesh and one in the spirit—the sooner they can understand that a choice exists between following Satan or following Jesus.

Acts 2:28 quotes David in the Old Testament foreseeing the coming of Christ to earth and thanking the coming of the Lord for imparting "The ways of life." David's use of the plural "ways" suggests that there must be at least two ways of seeing and living life. Someone once said that traveling by passenger train was like "looking at America with its back turned" because you saw things that you had never seen before, although they had existed all along. In contrast, interstate highways are constructed on the paths of least resistance because it's cost effective to go around a natural impediment. Therefore, an interstate highway may get you efficiently to your destination, but it will not take into account the scenic quality that you will encounter. A railroad train's route, on the other hand, will be scenic because it often doesn't divert around a natural impediment but will tunnel through it. Thus, traveling by train often gives the passenger an unseen view of America's natural beauty. Although this beauty has been there all along, a train passenger will often see this natural beauty for the first time. David's vision that Christ's coming to earth would reveal the different ways of looking at life is much like the difference between traveling by rail or by car. Both modes of transportation might get you to a destination, but their difference lies in where you will arrive and what your travels will reveal along the way.

God knew of your individual existence on earth before the foundation of the world and before your physical birth on earth; this means that you must have existed in another spiritual state before you had a physical body. It is the difference between living in these two different states of being that causes people not to realize—in David's words—"the ways of life." Your spiritual being didn't end when you were physically born on earth; it arrived on earth with your physical body. Even the ancient Greek philosophers asked: How does a newborn know how to cry? Their answer was because it has cried before in a previous spiritual life. Therefore, these two beings—the spiritual and the physical—both exist in you right now, although Satan would have you to believe that you only live in the physical world. While most nonbelievers selfishly only acknowledge the physical body, it is a major mistake to ignore your spiritual self because the true way—or essence of life—is only revealed through it. "For as many as are led by the Spirit of God, they are the sons of God. For ye have not received the spirit of bondage again to fear; but ye have received the Spirit of adoption, whereby we cry, Abba, Father" (Romans 8:14-15). That's why so many people miss the point of their own life; they rely on their physical body and Satan's selfish physical world to provide them with the truth. Life's true meaning cannot be told by the limited perception of the physical body's senses but only through the human heart. Even a dog's hearing is 10 times greater than ours. While nonbelievers might be so self-centered to think that their physical body—despite its limitations—is telling them the entire truth about their life, it is not. In fact, Satan's story about your life is not only incomplete, but it is also inaccurate.

The essence of life, as David is quoted in Acts 2:2, is not found in the limited reality of the physical world. The physical body supplies to you only the limited and selfish information that Satan wants you to know. In truth, something greater and more supernatural is happening in your physical self every day that you cannot perceive by ordinary human senses. This invisible something is your spiritual self living inside of your physical self while you are alive on earth. When your physical body dies, then your spiritual body moves on to one of two places: heaven or hell. Consequently, the true meaning and "ways of life" quoted in Acts 2:28 are only revealed by God to your spiritual being. "Everyone that is of the truth heareth my voice" (John 18:37). This creates the difference in how people live their lives; they either live it temporarily and selfishly in Satan's earthy here and now of their physical body or they live it eternally with Jesus in their spiritual body with their future sight on heaven. In Acts 2:2 David states that he prefers to live his life in his Spirit, and you should, too. If you follow David's example, God, Jesus, and the Holy Spirit will help you to discern unselfishly the way of spiritual truth about your own life and why God created you. Satan's physical world cannot and will not do this for you. "For I am persuaded, that neither death, nor life, nor angels, nor principalities, nor powers, nor things present, nor things to come, Nor height, nor depth, nor any other creature, shall be able to separate us from the love of God, which is in Christ Jesus our Lord" (Roman 8:38-39).

6. To Gain Strength

"There is unquestionably this instinct in me which belongs to the lower orders of creation." Henry David Thoreau, Walden Pond

John 6:63 states that "It is the spirit that quickenth; the flesh profiteth nothing: the words that I speak unto you, they are spirit, and they are life." Thus, John 6:63 is making a distinction between the importance of the physical body and the importance of the spiritual body. We are composed of two bodies; the physical body that we can see and the spiritual body that we cannot see. However, John makes it clear that we should nurture the spiritual body and not the physical body. "It is the spirit that quickeneth," he states. "Quickeneth" means to restore to life, return to life, or to revive to life. Thus, it is through the spiritual body that we will be reborn through salvation, and it is in a spiritual body that we will be transformed to live in heaven. The Spirit will live forever, while the physical body will not. The average life expectancy in the United States is about 80 years. However, the average life expectancy of the Spirit is forever; the Spirit does not have an expiration date or a shelf life. It will live for eternity with Jesus in Heaven. Living forever sounds a lot better than living a mere 80 years, so why don't more people accept Jesus' offer of spending eternity in the spirit with Him?

While most people hear Satan's call to concentrate on honing their physical body with workouts at the gym and with the latest dieting craze, few people read the Bible to find the spiritual strength they need for their souls. Jesus makes it evident in John 6:63 that improving the physical body "profiteth nothing." So, why does Satan have us admiring and fawning over the appearance of our physical self?

All my life I have been an "exercise nut" by punishing my physical body and thinking that I was doing myself good. For over twenty-five years and seven days per week, I ran five miles per day from 5am to 6am. Then, when I got older and my hips, knees, and my feet started to hurt me, I moved indoors to a gym and onto an elliptical machine. Yet, after many years and thousands of miles of exercise, I have still arrived at the same chronical age with the same physical ailments, if not more. In fact, during my first year of working out on the elliptical, I tore a tendon in my ankle, which led to wearing an orthopedic boot for six weeks, which led to a blood clot in my right leg, which led to two blood clots in my left and right lungs, which led to taking a blood thinner tablet every day for the remainder of my life. If I had not exercised, maybe none of the above scenario would have happened. But one thing is sure, as people age the physical benefits associated with exercise diminish. I believe that the Bible states it in Romans 8:12-13 "Therefore, brethren, we are debtors, not to the flesh, to live after the flesh. For if ye live after the flesh, ye shall die: but if ye through the Spirit do mortify the deeds of the body, ye shall live." Of course, when you're young and you still bounce when you fall instead of skid when you're older, exercise might be beneficial for a while; however, as you grow older, rigorous physical exercise can start to do you more harm than good. This is what happened to me, and God slowed my exercise routine down in a hurry. One day I was running five miles a day, and the next day I was in the hospital emergency room. So, why do people like me—as my former self—spend so much time exercising their body instead of exercising spirit by listening to their Holy Spirit and reading the Word of Jesus Christ in the Bible?

The answer to this question is also found in John 6:63. Because Jesus' words are spiritual, His words communicate only with the Spirit; therefore, only those people who have opened their hearts to their Holy Spirit within them can hear Jesus' words, while those people who remain with hardened hearts cannot. Because the words that Jesus speaks are spiritual, only those people attending to their Spirit will hear them. Others not attending to their Spirit because of Satan's interference won't hear them. Jesus says that His words are "life" because those people who hear them will receive them and hear Jesus' voice within them, thus extending their physical life into the spiritual life of eternity. So, if you can hear Jesus' voice and his words, you are communicating and strengthening your Spirit, which is that important holy part of you. "God is a Spirit: And they that worship him must worship him in spirit and truth" (John 4:24).

Some people only believe what they can physically see and believe only what they can physically hear. This is Satan at work, making you believe that life is only lived in the one-dimensional physical self. Therefore, even though some people might hear the voice of Jesus talking to them through their Holy Spirit, the interference of the spiritual message caused by Satan's physical world distracts them from following it. "He that hath no rule over his own spirit is like a city that is broken down, and without walls" (Proverbs 25:28). God—through Jesus—knows those people who are His; He—like Jesus—has known them since the foundation of the world. "And ye also shall bear witness because ye have been with me from the beginning" (John 5:270). Then, the question becomes how attentive and inclined are you to exercising your Spirit by listening, praying, and reading the Bible to hear the eternal voice of Jesus calling to you through your Holy Spirit?

7. To Find Comfort

"The foundations of man are not in matter, but in spirit." Ralph Waldo Emerson, Essay on Nature

I once verbally agreed to a teaching contract with a Dean from a community college. We agreed on an annual salary for a teaching contract in May for the following fall semester starting in September. In preparation for teaching full-time, between May and August I resolved my other commitments so that I could devote full time to teaching. A few days before the start of the fall semester, I went to the college's business office to sign my contract. Curiously, despite inquiring about it several times during the summer, my contract had not arrived in the mail at my house. Upon my last inquiry, I learned that the teaching contract was in the college's business office and was ready for my signature. However, when I reviewed the contract before signing it, I discovered that the teaching salary for the academic year was one-half of the agreed upon amount. In May we agreed to X, then on the contract in September the salary appeared as Y. I mentioned the discrepancy to the business office manager, and she told me to seek out the Dean. A few hours later, I was able to speak to the Dean about the salary discrepancy in the contract, and he denied ever verbally agreeing to the salary amount in our May conversation. Not only couldn't I pay my bills with the contract's salary amount, but I also couldn't believe that the Dean blatantly lied to me about the agreed upon salary. He thought that I would agree to the last-minute lower salary, and I later learned from a secretary at the school that he often pulled this bait-and-switch routine on many people to reduce the college's salary obligation to its faculty. This time, however, his plan did not work, for I told him that I wouldn't and couldn't accept the salary because it was now $4,000 below the poverty level. He responded by not following me down the hallway to convince me to change my mind, but just yelled, "Fine! There are plenty of other people who will work for that salary."

By his trickery, Satan likes to make many people think that they are being smart by lying and cheating to achieve their goals. In fact, while those people gloat in their worldly business victories by their charades intended to dupe others, they are committing their souls to the depths of hell by doing so. Ephesians 6:12 makes it clear that the battle in the world is not with other people but with Satan for your soul's destination, and by seemingly winning in the physical world by deceiving other people the deceiver is actually losing his soul to Satan because Satan has succeeded in influencing his behavior. "For we wrestle not against flesh and blood, but against principalities, against powers, against the rulers of darkness of this world, against spiritual wickedness in high places" (Ephesians 6:12). Therefore, when anyone deceives another person by evil means, he might be gaining an advantage with Satan in this world, but he is losing his soul in the next world by being unholy and by following Satan instead of listening to the comforting message of Jesus through the Holy Spirit.

8. To Find Hope

"I celebrate myself, and sing myself, And what I assume you shall assume, For every atom belonging to me as good belongs to you." Walt Whitman, Song of Myself

Fortunately, you have the option of living life in God's spirit instead of living life in Satan's physical world, that is, if you don't accept Satan's physical world of evil distractions. You can defy Satan and choose to live your life in the Spirit by heeding and following Jesus' voice through the Holy Spirit—the Comforter. "… when the Comforter is come whom I will send unto you from the Father…" (John 15:26). So, if you "feel" your "inner voice" calling to you, it is the voice of the Holy Spirit. Instead of following the immoral and outward thinking of a physical world under Satan's rule, you can step away from how the fallen world operates under Satan's authority and live inwardly by joining Jesus who lives in you through the Holy Spirit. "I will walk before the Lord in the land of the living" (Psalm 116:9).

I recently read an article in a magazine that stated that statistically that there are 100,000 other people in the world who could be your true love besides the person you have chosen. In other words, making a choice from the heart about who to marry didn't matter because you could have chosen 100,000 other people as well. The article reminded me of some friends who recently celebrated their 45th wedding anniversary. At the celebration, I asked them how they met. As it turns out, they met in the eighth grade while standing by a row of lockers in the hallway. It was the first day of the new school year, and they had never seen each other before. They both looked up at the same time and gazed into each other's eyes, and something struck their hearts, and they have been a couple ever since. They dated exclusively throughout middle school, high school, and college. Now, they have four children and eight grandchildren. I didn't mention the article to them that claimed that statistically they could have been just as happy with 100,000 other people. I'm sure that they didn't care or want to hear it; they are still as much in love today as they were on the day that their eyes first met. Their initial decision to be together was made for them from the heart when they first stared into each other's eyes, and nothing in the world could change it.

This is what happens when feelings stir the heart; nothing can interfere with the heart's hopefulness—not even the true love statistics of Satan's secular world. Frankly, this couple wouldn't care about the other 100,000 people that they could have chosen to spend their live with. They were satisfied with their heart's first choice. And this is how it happens when you hear the Holy Spirit's voice speaking to your heart from the divine source of Jesus. Suddenly, your life's perspective changes, and you feel different, and nothing else matters in the world because you have heard a holy messenger speaking to your heart, as clearly as the couple heard God speak love between them during that very first stare. Jesus' love for you strikes quick and convincing hope into you, and it's like nothing you have felt before because it's an invisible spiritual connection and conversation. "Give me understanding. And I shall keep thy law; yea, I shall observe it with my whole heart" (Psalm 119:34). Regardless of what the secular experts might say about true love, love speaks from the heart, and Jesus is love! The truth is the truth when it is felt in the heart, and Jesus is truth. "And ye shall know the truth, and the truth shall make you free" (John 8:32).

When Christ died on the cross for your past sins and was resurrected on the third day from death into life, he went to heaven to live with God. Then, He sent the Holy Spirit, The Comforter, to protect you during your stay while living in Satan's domain on earth. "And I will pray the Father, and he shall give you another Comforter, that he may abide with you forever" (John 14:16). Jesus conferred The Holy Spirit upon you to tell you through the Holy Spirit what correct moral choices to make, to protect you from Satan's sinful world, and to comfort and to give you hope in what you have to endure as a Christian living on earth. In heaven, of course, there will be peace, harmony, justice, and fairness, but until you reach heaven with Jesus, your spiritual life and its nourishment will be protected by Jesus through the Holy Spirit. By Jesus giving you the gift of the Holy Spirit and by you listening to the Holy Spirit's voice—His spiritual messenger within you in your heart—Jesus Christ has given you the option of becoming more holy by living in the Spirit rather than by living in Satan's physical world. Jesus said, "It is the spirit that quickeneth (changes you); the flesh profiteth nothing: the words I speak unto you are spirit, and they are life" (John 6:44).

That's right! it is possible for you to live in the Spirit with hope while still being alive in your physical body on Satan's earth because the voice that you are hearing inside of you is the voice of God and Jesus Christ telling you through the Holy Spirit that you now have an inner spiritual life and an option to Satan's outer physical world of madness and deceit. "The fear of the Lord is the beginning of wisdom: and the knowledge of the holy is understanding" (Proverbs 9:10). Your choice to live in the Spirit while still living in the physical and corrupt world of Satan is an important decision, for its hope will determine where your soul will travel after your physical death. If you choose to live in the Spirit with Jesus Christ, read the Bible, accept Jesus as your personal savior, and make Christian choices in your behavior on earth—despite the evil that exists while living in Satan's physical world, your soul after your physical death with travel to heaven as a spirit to be with Jesus for eternity. However, if you choose to follow the evil suggestions of Satan in a fallen world and ignore Jesus calling to you through your Holy Spirit's voice, then after your physical death your sinful earthly choices will drop your soul into the depths of hell, and this is exactly what Satan wants " I applied mine heart to know, and to search, and to seek wisdom, and the reason for things, and to know the wickedness of folly, even of foolishness and madness" (Ecclesiastes 7:25). Therefore, you can rely on the hope given to you by the Holy Spirit's comfort and guidance and on Jesus to guide you to your eternal destination.

9. To Understand How Sin Is Contagious

"When we love our sin then we are damned indeed." – Graham Green, The Power and the Glory

I once worked at a large state-supported university. The university had hundreds of professors and thousands of students. So, it was easy to get lost in that large of a place, and often good deeds as well as bad deeds went unnoticed. My introduction to the large campus happened a few weeks after my arrival. Two tenured faculty members didn't much like my confident attitude as a new teacher. New teaching members at the university were supposed to remain silent at department meetings. Although I had been teaching in higher education for over twenty years, and the nuances of academia were familiar to me, the two tenured faculty members still didn't want to hear my opinions. So, when it was evident that they could not verbally intimidate me into being quiet, they started to physically attack me in the hallways between the faculty offices. "For ye see your calling, brethren, how that not many wise men after the flesh, not many mighty, not many noble are called: But God hath chosen the foolish things of the world to confound the wise; and God hath chosen the weak things of the world to confound the things which are mighty;" (1Corinthians 1:26-27). Anytime that another faculty member was not present when they approached me in the hallway, they would veer into my direction and bump into me. At first, it was just a gentle bump, but then as the academic year progressed, they started to shove me and knock me off balance. One time, they both shoved me into a hallway wall. At group celebrations like at Student Honor's Banquets, they would intentionally bump into me from behind in crowed rooms. While the physical abuse was continuing, I received a letter of complaint from the English Department Chairperson about my unprofessional behavior witnessed and signed by the two tenured faculty members. They seemingly had witnessed many unprofessional behaviors on multiple occasions, and they recommended that I be fired. The Department Chairperson and I spoke, and I denied the allegations. Their tenured voices, however, carried more power than mine, yet after some investigation the Department Chairperson found that the allegations were untrue and that I was a good and professional teacher who was well-liked by my students, so she refused to fire me.

After that, the physical abuse in the hallways escalated and continued for over three years, with university officials looking the other way and/or refusing to believe it. The Department Chairperson did nothing to stop it after refusing to fire me, the Humanities Dean did nothing, and the Human Resource Department did nothing. It was as if evil could hide in plain sight at such a large university, where it was either accepted as normal behavior or too much trouble to investigate. And this is how Satan's sinful world works. Satan confuses people as to their moral obligation towards others. His world is about aggression and power; it's a world where civility and morality are void in favor of personal benefit. Thus, Christians in Satan's secular world must be prepared to defend themselves against aggression and immoral corruption in plain sight by seeking the comfort and safety of a personal spiritual relationship with Jesus Christ through the Holy Spirit.

Thus, it is your personal relationship with Jesus Christ that keeps your spiritually safe by helping you to understand sin by listening to your Holy Spirit that provides you with comfort and direction on earth in times of trouble and is your pathway to heaven after your physically die, and listening to Jesus calling to you through the Holy Spirit in your "inner voice" is your first step in building that personal and spiritual relationship with Jesus. "They which are the children of the flesh, these are not the children of God" (Romans 9:8). Therefore, it is simple. The implications of whether you choose to live your 80 years or so on earth in the physical body of Satan's here and now or choose to live in the hereafter for eternity in your spiritual body with Jesus will have serious implications for where your soul goes for eternity. If you chose to live in your outward physical self by accepting Satan's pursuits in the world and decline listening to the spiritual voice of your inner self, then you will go to hell. If, however, you chose to live your life in the spirit by understanding sin and listening and obeying the directions of your inner spiritual self through the voice of the Holy Spirit, then you will be on a spiritual path to salvation to go heaven to be with Jesus. "Then shall the dust return to the earth as it was: and the spirit shall return unto God who gave it" (Ecclesiastes 12:7).

Colossians 3:24 explains what is at stake for the destination of your soul by your actions on earth. These six words "... for ye serve the Lord Christ" so simply and eloquently states it all. After everything is said and done, and after your life is over, and after your earthly and physical death has occurred, what will then happen to you? Will you just cease to exist, as so much sinful and decaying flesh turned to dust buried in the ground? Or will your soul—your new spiritual life and being—be transformed and transported at the time of your death beyond the physical grave and into a spiritual and wonderful life with Jesus in heaven. The continuation of your life's story after your physical death depends on understanding your sinful nature and what to do about it during your present existence on earth. If you serve Satan, who is the master of deceit in his fallen world, and if you worship Satan's sinful idols of the physical world, which are the shrines of Satan's sinful disobedience to Jesus Christ, then you can rightfully expect your soul to land in hell. "Marvel not at this: for the hour is coming, in which all that are in the graves shall hear his voice and shall come forth; they that have done good, unto the resurrection of life, and they that have done evil, unto the resurrection of damnation" (John 5: 28-29).

Therefore, how you live your life on earth under Satan's control and the choices that you make while here will clearly determine your soul's destination after you die. The good news is that you currently have some control over where your soul lands, although most people won't think about their soul's eternal destination until it is too late. The cause-and-effect relationship between how they live now and where their soul will live later never enters most people's minds. Most people are too busy following Satan's distractions on earth to contemplate what their earthly actions will mean for their eternal destination. And this is the way Satan wants it; he likes it when people only concern themselves with their earthly desires. Satan doesn't want you to think about sin or anything else but yourself and fulfilling your earthly pursuits. That's why he puts so many distractions on earth for you to follow. Satan wants you to believe that you must get all your pleasure now on earth because nothing exists beyond it. But this is not true. In fact, everything exists beyond this world in heaven. When you are with Jesus in heaven, there will be no more: pain, suffering, strife, starvation, or grief. No more: anger, discouragement, or failure. No more: heartache, resentment, and fear. All these worldly defects now controlled by Satan's sinful systems on earth will be gone because in heaven everything is perfect. In fact, while there is no marriage in heaven, you will be reunited with other Christian family members and friends who have passed on before you, and you will all meet once again as spiritual souls of sparkling angelic light. "For when they shall rise from the dead, they neither marry, nor are they given in marriage; but are as the angels which are in heaven" (Mark 12:25). Imagine it! Life will finally be put morally right because you will be living in the household of God. Why someone wouldn't want to live forever in perfect peace and harmony is beyond me.

10. To Feel and Understand Your Need for Jesus

"I wonder if he is not afraid to be alone with himself." Nathaniel Hawthorne, The Minister's Black Veil.

Years ago, I took my cat Luther to the veterinarian for his annual checkup. It was a beautiful May morning, and the sun was shining into a new spring season to bring life to everything. The veterinarian's office was empty, so I was alone sitting while holding my cat Luther. Suddenly, the door opened, and a young woman entered carrying a miniature white poodle. She sat down in the waiting room chair close to me, and we remained in an awkward silence for a few minutes. Then, to break the silence into conversation, she related to me that it was her 33rd birthday. I wished her a happy birthday, and then she related something that she did every year on her birthday that made me feel uncomfortable. She said that after her poodle's veterinarian's visit today that she would be going to a photographer's studio to pose for nude photographs. She said that ever since she was seventeen years old that she had been keeping a yearly photographic chronicle of her body's aging. By itself, the nude photo shoot seemed to me like an unusual thing to do, much less to talk about it to a stranger, although what people do in the privacy of their own birthday suit wasn't any of my business. In short, I thought that if she wanted to have a chronicle of her aging process through a nude photographic rendition that it was her business and not mine. Then, she told me what she did with the photographs each year after they were taken. Every year after she received the prints of her nude photo-shoot from the photographer, she immediately had them framed and mounted them on her living room wall. By now, I felt that her telling me these details was a little more than I needed to know. I mean, how many people would relate such a personal story about themselves to a total stranger? To this day, I do not know if her story was true. Was she just telling me the story to get a reaction from me? I do not know. But one thing is for sure: some people do not have a sense of boundaries and propriety about their choice of topics for public discussion, although moral boundaries and self-control are critical to living in the Spirit and becoming a Christian because you must move beyond living a life in the adoration of the physical body into living a life in the adoration of Jesus in the spiritual body.

Therefore, a crucial part of becoming a follower of Jesus Christ is needing Him in a constant desire for seeking spiritual truth for self-improvement and seeking a lifestyle change to reject your physical body and to accept your spiritual body. You must be willing to listen to the Holy Spirit and to examine yourself and your behavior to move beyond living in your physical body towards living in your spiritual body. "It is not for you to know the times or the seasons, which the Father hath put in his own power. But ye shall receive power, after that the Holy Ghost is come upon you…" (Acts 1:7-8). Without admitting to Jesus and to yourself that you are falling short of your true self and that your thoughts and actions are often sub-standard, then you will not change from living in a physical body to living in a spiritual body. In short, you need Jesus' help in becoming aware of your own lifestyle flaws to make a spiritual change. "What fruit had ye then in those things whereof ye are now ashamed? For the end of those things is death. But now being made free from sin, and become servants of God, ye have your fruit unto holiness, and the end everlasting life. For the wages of sin is death; but the gift of God is eternal life through Jesus Christ our Lord" (Romans 6: 21-23). Only Jesus can help you to completely accept yourself as a spiritual being. If, however, you examine your heart and hear Jesus' voice through the Holy Spirit calling to you to make better lifestyle choices, then you can accept your need for Jesus and live as a spiritual body by turning away from your sinful physical life and walking into a different spiritual lifestyle direction, one that doesn't offend your holy self. "And now why tarriest thou? Arise, and be baptized, and wash away thy sins, calling on the name of the Lord" (Romans 22:16).

11. To Know Jesus' Healing Power

"Another flaw in the human character is that everybody wants to build and nobody wants to do maintenance." Kurt Vonnegut, Hocus Pocus

Many times, however, Satan prevents people from examining their own heart to conclude that they must change and need Jesus' help. Sometimes, when Satan exerts his influence on people, they see no need to change their behavior; thus, spiritual healing through Jesus cannot take place. Therefore, spiritual healing begins when a person realizes that they are spiritually ill and in need of spiritual healing because they hear their Holy Spirit—the voice of Jesus—calling to them. In 2 Corinthians 13:5, Paul's advice 2,000 years ago to the Corinthians to "examine yourselves, whether ye be in the faith…" was as accurate then as it is now. Feeling the spiritual need to change because of hearing Christ's voice calling you through the Holy Spirit is essential in revealing the flaws in yourself. It is an important first step in moving away from living in your previous physical self to living in your spiritual self and toward being spiritually healed by Jesus. The combination of hearing the voice of the Holy Spirit telling you to change, then having the desire for self-examination in order to accept change, and then feeling the application of the forgiving grace of Jesus working in you to change all combine to provide a spiritual path to Jesus. "Fear thou not; for I am with thee: be not dismayed; for I am thy God: I will strengthen thee; yea, I will help thee; yea, I will uphold thee with the right hand of righteousness" (Isaiah 41:10).

Many years ago, when I was a 15-year-old little league baseball player, I was coached by two brothers who were Christians, a fact that I found out the hard way. The previous week, I had gone three hits for three times at bat and helped to score the winning run in the bottom of the ninth inning. Yet, despite my heroics during the previous week's game, the Christian coaches made me sit the bench for the first seven innings during the next week's game. While sitting out the first 7 innings of the game on the bench, I was furious. What coach benched their star player? So, just before the start of the eighth inning I asked one of the coaches why I had been benched? He told me that he wanted to give all players a chance to play in the game. I sat back down on the bench until the warm-ups for the eighth inning began, when the coaches finally sent me in to play my position at first base. By now, our team was losing 16 to 2, and I was distracted so much by the score and by being made to sit on the bench for seven innings that I had made up my mind to quit the team after the game.

While deep in my thoughts of retribution about quitting the team after the game, I wasn't paying attention during the warm-ups, and I accidently put my right hand into the baseball glove too soon to practice a double play relay to second base, and the baseball hit the top of my right hand thumbnail and torn back my thumbnail. Blood gushed from my thumb, and my dad, who was watching the game from the bleachers, immediately took me to the emergency room at the hospital. The young doctor at the emergency room took out a pair of tiny scissors from a stainless-steel medicine cabinet and approached me. My father asked him if he was going to "freeze" my thumb before using the scissors to cut beneath the length of my thumbnail to remove the dangling piece of the nail. The young doctor said that it wasn't necessary to numb the thumb, and he began to cut down under my thumbnail. My screams didn't seem to bother him, as he nonchalantly continued to cut halfway down and under my thumbnail with my blood gushing everywhere. My father, who was kind of fascinated by the doctor's approach, remained silent. "Brethren, if a man be overtaken in a fault, ye which are spiritual, restore such a one in the spirit of meekness; considering thyself, lest thou also be tempted" (Galatians 6:1).

To make a long story short, the doctor successfully cut off the remaining piece of thumbnail and bandaged up my wound. His parting words still echo in my ears, "I'm afraid your baseball career is over for the remainder of this season." In short, I wouldn't even get a chance to get revenge against the coaches by quitting the team for being benched. By now, what was the point: I would be lost for the entire baseball season anyway because of the injury to my thumb. "He that troubleth his own house shall inherit the wind" (Proverbs 11:29).

After the injury, I never played little-league summer baseball again, and it wasn't until 55 years later that I fully appreciated the Christian attitude of the coaches for insisting that all players entered the game. Whether they were good players or bad players really didn't matter; because of Christian fairness everybody played in the game. However, at the time that I was sitting on the bench, I was an unchristian 15-year-old kid and not wise enough to examine myself or the motives of the coaches for sitting me on the bench to let everybody else play. And over the years, I have examined and re-examined this baseball game and its meaning to me. I've concluded that Jesus saved me from the embarrassment of quitting the baseball team, so He took me out of the game Himself and benched me for not understanding the Christian motives regarding the decency in the coaches' decision. After this baseball game, reflection and self-examination about my life's experiences gradually became an essential part of my life, and years later it was in this evaluative state of mind that Jesus awakened me to the Holy Spirit within me.

However, today—whether young or old—many people aren't interested in examining themselves to experience the healing power of Jesus in them to make a change that leads to a personal relationship with Jesus Christ. Satan doesn't allow them enough time to think about living in their Spirit. Satan doesn't want people to think spiritually; he wants them to think physically about what they can experience and possess. He especially wants people to think that they can be happy by owning material possessions. Thus, Satan controls people by immersing them in self-indulgent behavior in the physical world to keep them busy. Satan knows that he can fool most people into thinking that they are happy by giving them enough possessions and power. This self-absorption and over-indulgence dupes most secular people into feeling satisfied and sleepy unto the needs of their Spirit; it's Satan way of lulling them into an earthly delusional state. Therefore, Satan does not want you to think about your soul, your sinful lifestyle, the clock ticking, or about the healing power of Jesus; he just wants you to believe that you need to work harder to get more superficial stuff. By the way, there is no end to wanting more stuff. Wanting more stuff simply leads to wanting more stuff. Don't be fooled by Satan's delivery system for your life as an endless and mindless pursuit of wanting more stuff instead of pursuing the healing power of Jesus through the Spirit. But remember, if you accept Satan's delivery system for your life's meaning as being predicated solely on what you own and you can't take your stuff with you after you die, then what does that leave you with? That's right! It leaves you with nothing.

Long ago, I knew a brother and sister who were waiting patiently for the reading of their recently deceased mother's will. Their mother had owned a huge farmhouse in the Midwest, and her house was full of expensive antiques. Both siblings knew that someone would get the house and the property to sell, and someone would receive the antiques. As much as the house and property were worth, both had concluded that the antiques were worth much more. On the day before the reading of their mother's will, her daughter announced to her bother that she had seen the will in advance. She noted that her seeing the will happened totally by accident. She explained that she had been in the attorney's office on the previous day, and they were discussing the time of the reading of the will when he was momentarily called out of his office by his secretary, at which time he had left their mother's will open on his desk in full view. Of course, she read it, although she was supposed to avert her eyes, and she learned that she was the recipient of the antiques, so she had acquired a rental truck that morning to load all the antiques that afternoon and drive them back to her house in Rhode Island from Michigan. That afternoon, her brother helped her to load all the antiques into the rental truck, and with a rather crisp goodbye she waved out the driver's side window and drove away.

On the next day, the brother dutifully arrived at the attorney's office at 10am for the reading of their mother's will, only to find out that he—and not his sister—had been left all the antiques by his mother's will and that his sister had been left the house and the property. So now, the sister not only owned the house and the property, but she was also in possession of all the antiques and by now had driven across four state lines headed to her house in Rhode Island. Therefore, the son was left with nothing from his mother's will except the ill-will for his sister with whom he has not spoken to for over thirty years.

Thus, making what you own the premise of your life's meaning is not a good investment of your time on earth. Of course, Satan wants you to believe that taking the time to own physical things is the only and most powerful investment in life. Yet, many people upon their deathbed openly regret the morbid self-interest displayed in their life by their pursuit of money and power instead of paying more attention to the healing properties of Jesus for their soul. In the end, your net worth isn't calculated in monetary terms; money doesn't mean anything to God. In the end, He only wants to know if you had a personal investment in the healing power of His Son Jesus Christ and whether Jesus is your personal Lord and Savior. Everything else in life is temporary trash devised by Satan to keep you busy.

12. To Know What's Valuable

"New knowledge is the most valuable commodity on earth. The more truth we have to work with, the richer we become." Kurt Vonnegut, Breakfast of Champions

In calculating your life's net worth by what you own, you also miss the most important asset in your life—your Spirit. By involving your soul into your net worth's calculation, you will discover that your life's meaning is more valuable than any material possession because it extends your existence beyond this world and into the next. By asking the more important spiritual questions about your life, Jesus and the Holy Spirit will provide you with the proper numbers for calculating your life's value. You are not solely the sum of your physical possessions; your spiritual worth to God is more paramount than that. Satan's physical possession calculation of your net worth is just his earthly way of making wrong seem right. In short, Satan wants you to believe that this physical world is all you have to evaluate yourself; he wants you to march in lock step in the parade of the walking dead with other unthinking souls who are making their way slowly to hell. Don't buy into it! Satan's equation for your life's value based on what you materially own is pathetic. It's a dead end.

When I was a senior in college, I rented a beach house on Lake Superior with six other students. It was a ranch house twenty feet from the water's edge, and it had a three-seasons porch overlooking the lake. I liked the windowed, three-seasoned porch because it could be used when the cold weather approached. One day, I remember sitting in my favorite chair on the porch in November while studying for an American Literature exam when a violent storm off the lake forced me into the living room. At first, the waves from Lake Superior just lapped upon the shore close to the house. Then, an hour later the waves started hitting the lower portion of the living room picture window. Then an hour later, the waves were splashing mid-way up the living room picture window, and then one hour later the waves where hitting the top of the picture window, and at that time, I headed back to the rear of the house to my room where I knew the house was moored into more solid ground.

The next morning revealed a calm lake, sunshine, and warmer temperatures for November. I went outside to examine the house to see if there was any damage. To my surprise, the large waves from the Lake Superior storm had eaten the sand beach almost entirely away from under the house. Only about one-quarter of the sand beach was left under the house. The remainder of beach still under the house was located at the portion furthest from the lake. To my horror, I also discovered that the three-seasons porch was missing—that the large waves from Lake Superior had ripped the porch away from the house and taken it out to sea. The steel pilings under the house that held it into place were clearly exposed. In short, the house with me in it was almost washed out to sea.

I telephoned the landlord, and he drove over to the house. The minute he saw the house, he jumped out of his car and started waving his arms in disbelief. He had invested all his self-worth into his rental properties, and the lake's damage to this rental house was almost like someone had punched him in the nose or given him a blackeye. It was evident that he had not invested any time into seeking the Lord Jesus. If he had, he would have known that the house was not a factor in estimating his personal net worth. He, personally, had a spiritual value as well, while the ownership of a house was only an earthly possession. They were two separate calculations. Yet, there he was taking it personally, as if the storm had almost drowned him instead of his house.

With the examination of your earthly behavior, as provided by listening to the voice of the Holy Spirit, you will begin to discover that your behavior is unbecoming of your true self. Therefore, it is the depth of your true spiritual self that you seek, and only through Jesus Christ can you begin to recognize the value of yourself. "Know ye not your own selves, how that Jesus is in you…" (2 Corinthians 13:5). So, the first step—and a crucial one—is having both a desire and a need to become a Child of God by reflecting on your true value as a spiritual person by listening to your Holy Spirit and then reconciling it with how you are living your life. Without taking the first step towards discovering the value of your holiness by listening to Jesus in your heart through your Holy Spirit, you cannot begin the second step of praying to Jesus for forgiveness, reading the Bible, and admitting to Him that you are a sinner and in need of His redemptive grace. If you truly seek forgiveness and commit to following a righteous pathway to God, then each successive prayerful conversation with Jesus will help you to move closer in your personal spiritual relationship with Christ and to the true value of why you were put on earth by God. Jesus said, "I am the way, the truth, and the life: no man cometh unto the Father, but by me (John 14:6).

13. To Protect Your Soul

"I believe in Christianity as I believe that the sun has risen; not only because I see it, but because by it I see everything else." —CS Lewis

The primary difference between the physical and the spiritual body lies in from where the power in each realm derives. The power in the physical body—as we have discussed—comes from Satan. The power in the spiritual body comes from God. So, there are two bodies within you, and both bodies are coming from two conflicting power sources and two conflicting points of view. Of course, Satan wants your earthly body to take control over your spiritual body; that's why he dangles possessions and power as distractions in front of you. Basically, he wants to distract you long enough to have you forget about also having a spiritual body." But, beloved, remember ye the words which were spoken before of the apostles of our Lord Jesus Christ; How that they told you there should be mockers in the last time, who should walk after their own ungodly lusts. These be they who separate themselves, sensual, having not the Spirit" (Jude 17-19). By contrast, the spiritual body's presence is comprised of the power of God working inside of you as a "feeling" that you are moving closer to your spiritual self and closer to having a personal relationship with Jesus by rejecting Satan's corrupt temptations in the physical world.

These two conflicting power sources and whether to live in the physical or the spiritual body create a battle within you for the control of your soul. In every moment of every day in your life, there is a war going on inside of you; you are a holy combatant in a fierce firefight every day over who gains control of your soul. It is a battle to walk with Jesus to gain control of your spiritual self by rejecting Satan evil choices in the world. Whenever you make any decision, you morally side with either God or the Devil. The battle for the heaven or hell destination of your soul has been raging ever since Adam and Eve disobeyed God and picked the forbidden fruit (apple) from the Tree of Life. Of course, Satan told them that if they picked the apple that they, too, would instantly become gods. Satan told them that God didn't want them to pick the apple because God was jealous and didn't want any competition. Today, Satan still uses this same argument in the world to convince you that you can become your own little god by accumulating enough money and power. In short, money and power have now become today's evil apples because they make people worship wealth and possessions as idols. Therefore, while Jesus is explaining to you through the quiet voice of your Holy Spirit to get to know Him by improving yourself morally and spiritually by reading His Word in the Bible to join Him for eternity, Satan is on earth's street corner with a megaphone blasting his message to buy excessively and to live immorally for the here and now because there is no tomorrow. As you can see, there is quite a difference between the approaches and the perspectives used by both power sources. Yet, "Keep yourselves in the love of God, looking for the mercy of our Lord Jesus Christ unto eternal life" (Jude1:21).

Many years ago, I was sitting in my office when the English Department secretary entered and told me that there was an FBI agent waiting to speak to me. I said, "FBI?" "Yes," she continued, "complete with a 38 Caliber handgun on her hip." The FBI agent entered my office, sat down, and told me that a letter with my signature on it had been discovered in a file cabinet of a suspected felon who had been under FBI investigation and was now going to trial. She told me the name of the company where my letter had been found, and I explained to her that I had answered an advertisement in a reputable trade magazine about a small press being for sale. That was all there was to it, I explained, and purchasing the company had been financially risky, so I didn't make an offer. "That may be," she explained, "but the owners are now going to trial for fraud, and you may be called as a material witness, so be at the Louisville, Kentucky courthouse at 9am on Monday morning." "But I have classes to teach on Monday; I can't just leave and spend the entire weekend driving across three states to testify at a trial that I know nothing about." "That might be the case," she said, "but you better be there anyway, or get served with a contempt of court citation."

The FBI agent had arrived at my office on a Tuesday morning, and luckily by Friday morning I was notified that the defendants had entered into plea agreement with the prosecution so that there wouldn't be a trial on Monday. Yet, out of nowhere, because of Satan I had suddenly become a material witness for the prosecution in a FBI federal court case, so it is easy to understand why Satan's messaging gets the attention of so many people in the world; he owns all the evil world's systems, and he can utilize them at any time to try to disrupt the soul. Therefore, in a world control by the Evil One, your soul needs the protection of Jesus Christ.

14. To Find Your Holiness

"The closer you live to God, the smaller everything else appears." — Rick Warren, The Purpose Driven Life

Living life in the physical body means that you have bought into Satan's delusion that what you see in the world is all you get, and you had better get as much as you can for yourself because life is short. However, people living in the spiritual body know that something important is missing in life and that life is more complicated than what's physically seen at first glance, and this is certainly true when it comes to discerning your spiritual being. The Holy Spirit's voice and Jesus' presence in your life is real and a singular and holy event; thus, it can only be felt by you. Trying to explain "the feeling" to other nonbelievers is futile. They won't understand what's happening to you because they do not hear the voice of their own Holy Spirit calling in them. Thus, the experience of the Holy Spirit's involvement in your life is a personal one. And understanding the depths of your relationship with Jesus Christ through the Holy Spirit can only be experienced by you. "That he would grant you, according to the riches of his glory, to be strengthened with might by his Spirit in the inner man" (Ephesians 3:16). In short, the Holy Spirit only talks to the spirit, and the Holy Spirit only works through the Spirit. Therefore, discerning how the Spirit is at work within you through a holy messenger will only be experienced by you, and it is only happening to you because God wants only you to listen to Him and to follow his instructions. "If a man love me, he will keep my words: and my Father will love him, and we will come unto him, and make our abode with him" (John 14:23). Thus, only by asking questions of a spiritual nature and by seeing life through your personal and spiritual Eyes of Understanding can you begin to understand the spiritual depth of your own holy self. Currently, you are living in two worlds simultaneously: one promises the hope of a spiritual calling of an eternal life and the other the hopelessness of a physical death.

In 2 Corinthians 10:7, Paul writes to the people of Corinth because they seemed to be satisfied with the superficial meaning of living life in their physical self. However, by not living life in the Spirit, as provided by Jesus Christ, they will never understand the unholiness of their own existence. "… but they measuring themselves by themselves, and comparing themselves among themselves, are not wise" (2 Corinthians 10:12). According to Paul, if we ask questions and seek knowledge about Christ and our salvation, then we begin to understand our holy relationship with God and we begin to understand our life's true holy nature. Therefore, even the ancient Corinthians 2000 years ago believed mistakenly in themselves and the entertainment quality of Satan's world, but the people of Corinth were wrong then, and we are wrong now. God did not put us on earth to simply chase money to please ourselves.

Satan's money chase to buy possessions in the physical world is a shallow life's pursuit, and one that will not satisfy a spiritual person who seeks the true nature about their existence. Only through having a personal relationship with Jesus Christ and knowing Him as your personal Lord and Savior can you begin to understand the gravity of your holiness. "That Christ may dwell in your hearts by faith; that ye, being rooted and grounded in love, May be able to comprehend with all the saints what is the breadth, and length, and depth, and height; And to know the love of Christ, which passeth knowledge, that ye might be filled with all the fulness of God" (Ephesians 3:17-19). By entering into a spiritual relationship with Jesus Christ, you can begin to understand how life truly works—not as Satan wants you to see it work—but as how God reveals to you how it works. Finding your holiness is a spiritual passageway found only through Jesus Christ. Jesus is your spiritual guide to enlightenment and your spiritual connection to God.

To aid you in your spiritual journey, Jesus has given you the Holy Spirit as a guide and Comforter. He imparted the Holy Spirit to be your Comforter so that you could live life in your spiritual body and not in your physical body, although we are confined temporarily in a physical body on Satan's earth. By doing so, Jesus acknowledged that you would have problems when living in the Spirit while still living in Satan's domain on earth, but the Holy Spirit will always be there to provide you with spiritual comfort and guidance. "And I will pray the Father, and he shall give you another Comforter that he may abide with you for ever; Even the Spirit of truth; whom the world cannot receive, because it seeth him not, neither knoweth him: but ye know him; for he dwelleth with you, and shall be in you. I will not leave you comfortless: I will come to you" (John 16-18). So, the Holy Spirit was imparted to you by Jesus as a holy gift and as a promise from God to help and to deliver spiritual peace and understanding to you in a world often fraught with Satan's evil. Thus, believers can pray to Jesus and to the Holy Spirit for direction when they become confused and feel threatened by the circumstances in Satan's evil world. "For he that soweth to his flesh shall of the flesh reap corruption; but he that soweth to the spirit shall of the spirit reap life everlasting" (Galatians 6:8).

15. To Find Faith

"Faithless is he that says farewell when the road darkens." JRR Tolkien, The Fellowship of the Ring

Whether you live in the physical body or live in the spiritual body is sometimes difficult to understand. Some people never hear the voice of God through the Holy Spirit calling to them to repent. Those people who don't hear their inner voice of the Holy Spirit calling to them have Satan to blame for their deafness. Satan has made them hard of hearing and has hardened their heart to the point where they can no longer hear their Spirit's voice calling to them from within themselves." Ye stiffnecked and uncircumcised in heart and ears, ye do always resist the Holy Ghost as your fathers did, so do ye "(Acts 7:51). Satan's noise in the world makes it difficult for nonbelievers to listen to their Holy Spirit, yet God gets his message through to some people who He knows will hear Him, and when you start to hear the voice of God in you, you know and feel who is calling to you." For we through the Spirit wait for the hope of righteousness by faith" (Galatians 5:5).

Having faith and hearing Jesus' voice calling within you through the Holy Spirit is very difficult because we rely on our physical senses to perceive everything, yet hearing the Holy Spirit calling to you requires of you to have faith in what you are hearing without using your senses to know Jesus in your heart. "Now faith is the substance of things hoped for, the evidence of things not seen" (Hebrews 11:1). So, to know Jesus you must have faith, and to hear the Holy Spirit you must have an open heart to receive it. Only God can give you faith by awakening a longing in you to know Him and His Son Jesus. It is a supernatural event that goes beyond perception through the human senses and goes into God's realm of supernatural communication. But one thing is for sure: without first believing that there is a God, you will never have faith. "But without faith it is impossible to please him: for he that cometh to God must believe that he is…" (Hebrews 11:6). So, you can't smell faith, touch faith, hear faith, or see faith. Yet somehow God supernaturally enters your heart and soul to communicate it to you. However, in Paul's case coming to faith was different. Paul saw a flash of light at mid-day and heard Jesus' voice speaking to him. But for most of us, we come to have faith in God, His Son Jesus, and in the indwelling Holy Spirit in more subtle ways. With faith, seeing is not believing, and believing is by not seeing.

If faith had a scent and man could smell it, faith could be found by just following your nose. Faith, of course, would have the sweet-smelling aroma of a bakery making donuts at 4am because Jesus wants people to be enamored by its hypnotic aroma.

If you could touch faith, God wouldn't make faith rough and jagged; it would be smooth so that anyone could easily glide their fingers across it without harm. Faith wouldn't be hot; it would be warm and inviting to the touch so that no one who touched Faith would want to take their hand away.

If you could hear faith, it would be a musical composition of perfect pitch and perfect rhythm, and it would be an unforgettable melody like some pieces of classical music that go straight to the heart. If you could hear Faith, it would be a song so pleasant that you would hum its melody for the rest of your life.

If you could see faith, it would have its own color, and not one found on the color spectrum, and it would be the most pleasant sight ever seen.

Once you saw faith, you wouldn't be able to take your eyes away from it. Faith as sight would be a can't-believe-your-eyes phenomenon; it would appear so magical and mysterious that you couldn't look away. And that is the point: Faith is both supernaturally magical and mysterious because it eludes the human senses. It is God's way of communicating with us in His supernatural way.

Years ago, when I was in the army, I went to a sergeant's house to watch a Saturday afternoon football game. It was supposed to be a close college game. Yet, the football game provided far less excitement than what happened after it. I was in the kitchen rummaging through the refrigerator looking for something to eat, when I saw a cat bowl filled with cat food on the kitchen floor. When the sergeant joined me in the kitchen, I said, "I never knew that you had a cat." "Well, it's my wife's cat, and it's not very friendly; he only comes out late at night to eat. We know that he's still alive because the food bowl is empty in the morning." "So, you never see your cat?" I asked. "That's right," he said. "We haven't seen him for two years. He hides in the house during the daylight hours, and then he sneaks out in the middle of the night to eat." "Let's go find him," I said.

We searched for the cat in the sergeant's house for over one hour with the sergeant continuously warning me to be careful if we found the cat. "He doesn't much like people; the only person that he can tolerate is my wife." Just then, we opened one of two doors on a built-in cabinet on a wall in a spare bedroom. At first, I remember seeing the cabinet door swinging slowly open and then seeing the shelves of the built-in cabinet holding spare blankets and sheets. I took note of a yellow blanket on the top shelf, and then I saw the cat leaping from the yellow blanket towards my face. I did not have time to react; it was all over in a fraction of a second. The cat had scored a technical knockout on me with a flurry of sharp scratches to my face. The following week, I had to explain to friends and family how I had been TKO'd by a ten-pound Tabby Cat named Fluffy.

Likewise, going out of your way to look for faith in all the wrong places and for the wrong reasons can also be harmful. If you try to find faith by looking outward by rummaging through all the painful closets of your own life, you will fail because faith gives hope and not despair. If there was ever any doubt about how faith works supernaturally in a

Christian's heart and about how the dead who live in Christ meet their end, it is forever explained in 1 Thessalonians 4: 13-18. In that scripture, Paul makes it clear that the living should not be ignorant about the fate of those people who die as Christians. "But I would not have you to be ignorant, brethren, concerning them which are asleep (dead), that ye sorrow not, even as others which have no hope" (1 Thessalonians 4:13). So, Paul states that there is a difference between how a saved believer in Jesus and a non-believer accepts death, and having faith is the difference. Because the non-believer does not have faith or hope; death is final. But, according to Paul and scripture, the believer should "sorrow not" because there is something more to life beyond physical death, and death is not final. And Paul wants to make sure that Christians reading Thessalonians understand the difference that faith makes because even those Christians who have died previously will be raised from the dead unto life through believing in Jesus. "For if we believe that Jesus died and rose again, even so them also which sleep (are dead but believed in Jesus) will God bring with him" (1 Thessalonians 4:14). So, the promise of being resurrected from a physical body into a spiritual body when we die not only pertains to those Christians who are currently alive, but also extends to those Christians who have previously died. "For the Lord himself shall descend from heaven with a shout, with the voice of the archangel, and with the trump of God: and the dead in Christ shall rise first" (1 Thessalonians 4:16). Therefore, those souls who have previously died and have faith in the resurrection of Jesus Christ have been raised from the grave into spiritual life, as well as those Christians with faith and hope still alive on earth. "Then we which are alive and remain shall be caught up together with them in the clouds, to meet the Lord in the air: and so shall we ever be with the Lord" (1 Thessalonians 4:17). What a glorious day for all Christians when "We ... shall be caught up together" (Thessalonians 4:17).

Therefore, all Christians have this one hope, one faith, and one calling that will be realized by meeting Jesus one day upon their own spiritual resurrection. Hence, physical death is not the end of life for a Christian; it is the faithful beginning of a new spiritual life with Lord Jesus in heaven. Jesus' resurrection defeated death by His overcoming the grave and coming back to life, and thereby made it possible for Christians to do the same. What is buried in the ground at the gravesite is not the essence of you; it is only the physical vessel that contained your soul, and when your physical body dies, your Holy Spirit (the Comforter) is released from your physical body to bring forth your new spiritual self to God. In the meantime, and while you are still living in our physical body on earth, the Holy Spirit was sent by Jesus to be a Comforter amid the travails of Satan's earthly world. But when your physical body dies, it will no longer contain your Spirit, and you will be released from your physical body as a spiritual being into a new spiritual body and life with Jesus. This is how physical death and faith in Jesus Christ works for a Christian, and Paul reminds all Christians in 1 Thessalonians, including us today, to take comfort by this transformation from physical death into spiritual life. "Wherefore, comfort one another with these words" (1 Thessalonians 4:18).

CHAPTER THREE

30 LIFESTYLE CHOICES TO NURTURE YOUR SPIRITUAL SELF

"I love you as a sheriff searches for a walnut

That will solve a murder case unsolved for years."

Kenneth Koch, poem To You

1. Buy a Bible and Read It

When attending church, you will find that there aren't any perfect Christians. Christians are flawed humans like everyone else living among the many temptations of Satan's sinful world, but Christians know what God expects them to do as a child of God by reading the Bible to combat Satan, and they try every day to do what is right by God by taking the fight for their soul to Satan. It's true that sometimes they fail and fall, but at least they know that they are in a fight against Satan for their spiritual life. By reading the Bible, meditating on the scripture, putting the moral Word of God into action in their daily life, by praying, and by attending church, they are doing what they can to stand "But they that wait upon the LORD shall renew their strength; they shall mount up with wings as eagles; they shall run, and not be weary; and they shall walk, and not faint" (Isaiah 40:31).

To start to fight for your soul against Satan, this is what you can do. If you don't own a Bible, go to a bookstore and buy one because the Bible's words contain "… The sword of the Spirit, which is the word of God" (Ephesians 6:17). God doesn't care about how much you pay for your Bible; His concern is that you purchase one and read it. I go to the book section in the discount stores. If you go to the discount section, you will find that the cheapest book on the bookshelf is the Bible. I guess this is a comment about Satan's priorities in the world. A cheap price in Satan's world of consumerism usually doesn't mean a better product. But in this case, it does. In fact, the Bible might be the least expensive book on the shelf, but spiritually it is also the most expensive and valuable book on earth. Without reading the Bible, you will not know in your heart how to live as a Christian life. Without reading the Bible, you will not know in your heart that you have a savior in Jesus Christ. Without reading the Bible, you will not know in your heart that God loves you. Without reading the Bible, you will not know in your heart that you have a Holy Spirit given to you by Jesus Christ. Without reading the Bible, you will not know in your heart that you are a spiritual being as well as a physical being. You get my point: Without reading the Bible, you will not know fully about what God expects of you and intends for your life. The essential and supernatural message about who you are and why you exist is found in the Bible. The Bible is God's direct Word informing you about yourself. "Search the scriptures; for in them ye think ye have eternal life and they are they which testify of me" (John 5: 39).

I bought my current King James Version of the Bible for $1 over fifteen years ago, and God's Word in it is just as accurate as in any other more expensive Bible. How much you pay for your Bible is up to you. When you attend church, look around at the Bibles that other people carry. Some are expensive leather-bound Bibles with leather carrying cases. Yet really, I don't think God thinks that people are more holy because of how much they pay for their Bible. There are much larger moral principles on which to decide a person's holiness. The importance of a Bible lies in just owning, reading, and meditating on it. As you will soon discover, there are also many versions of the Bible. Therefore, before buying a Bible investigate which Bible best suits your needs by reading a little of it. If you understand God's message to you clearly, then it's the right Bible for you. I chose the King James Version of the Bible published in 1611 because I like the beautiful word choice translation, while other people may find a modern language version and translation of the Bible with more contemporary word choice more to their liking. "But whoso keepeth his word, in him verily is the love of God perfected: hereby know we that we are in him" (1 John 2:5).

As previously stated, Satan's physical world is very loud, and Satan's external noise can block out your ability to hear the voice of your Holy Spirit. Finding a quiet place to read and to reflect daily on your Bible is a pleasant soulful experience. However, finding a quiet place so that you can read the Bible, meditate on its verses, and pray to Jesus is not high on Satan's priority list of things for you to do. Therefore, expect Satan to try to interfere and interrupt your quiet time with God. To avoid missing too many days each week, I keep a Bible reading journal where I simply record the Bible chapters and verses read that day and the date. In this way, I keep myself on my personal spiritual journey despite Satan's interruptions. Satan will try to interrupt your Bible reading time; you can count on it. He'd like you to believe that you have more important things to do in life, but you don't. Your cell phone will ring with an unexpected caller. You'll suddenly remember that you forgot to do something yesterday. Disruptive thoughts will intrude on your reading concentration and impair comprehension. Over the years, I've identified these interruptions and many others as Satan trying to reduce the quality and the amount of time that I spend contemplating and meditating on the Word of God.

You, too, need to be aware of Satan's distractions. You don't have anything more important to do in life than to read your Bible and to pray to Jesus for moral direction and for the salvation of your soul. Being saved by Jesus is the greatest gift that you can ever receive in your life. "For God so loved the world, that he gave his only begotten Son, that whosoever believeth in him should not perish, but have everlasting life" (John 3:16). By comparison, other things in life are meaningless. For instance, you could have the largest yacht in the world, but what good is it if you can't sail it into heaven? You could have all the money in the world, but what good is it if you can't take it with you when you die? When you die the only currency that's important to Jesus Christ is whether you chose to live in the Spirit with Him as a good Christian instead of living in the physical world and accepting Satan's corruption. Right now, God, Jesus, and the Holy Spirit want to spend some supernatural time with you to expand your spiritual awareness to protect you from Satan's grasp. Guided by The Holy Trinity—God, Jesus, and the Holy Spirit—and by reading the Bible, praying, and attending church, you can overcome the sinful influences of Satan's world by nurturing a stronger spiritual you.

2. Learn to Listen

"It takes two to speak the truth—one to speak and another to listen." Henry David Thoreau, A Week on the Concord and Merrimack Rivers

Revelation 3:20 is such a powerful verse in scripture because it is Jesus Christ's promise to us that he will give us salvation and what we need in this life to overcome Satan's temptation and to keep God's ways. "Behold, I stand at the door, and knock…" (Revelation 3:20). The door at which Jesus stands and knocks is not the door of a house, but at the spiritual door of your heart where He awaits. By knocking on your spiritual door, Jesus is calling to you; He is calling to you to alert you to

His appearance. When someone knocks at a door, it is an alerting sound of someone's presence who awaits recognition. Jesus is no different; He is waiting for you to recognize His presence in your life and for you to hear his appeal by knocking on the door of your heart. "… open the door, I will come into him," (Revelation 3:20). Therefore, Jesus will enter your heart if you will just hear Him calling to you and let him enter. Acknowledging Christ's presence in you is a heart and soul issue, and Jesus will continue His knocking, but you must listen for His presence at your heart's door.

Someone once told me that you can't learn anything by talking; you can only learn new things by listening. And it's true, isn't it? For example, if you are talking all the time, you are only saying what you already know, and you're not going to learn anything new by the utterance of your own words. For example, I know some people who call me on the telephone and talk so much and so fast that I can't get a word in "edgewise." But then, it occurred to me that these people didn't telephone me to listen to me; they telephoned me to hear the sound of their own voice and to utter what they already knew. In a way, it's self-serving and selfish. Someone telephones me not to listen to what I have to say, but to listen to the sound of their own voice and what it has to say. Therefore, the question becomes: Why did they even bother to telephone me in the first place, when they could have just talked to themselves at home?

I once had an eighty-three-year-old aunt who talked so much that she appeared to be choking and suffocating on her own words. One time, I sat quietly and listened to her talk without stopping for one hour and seventeen minutes. It was supposed to be a two-way conversation, and although I was sitting just across the table from her, she continued to talk to me as if I were invisible. I remember watching her gasping for air between long sentences like her head was being held underwater. She was particularly long-winded when she spoke about her kidney ailments, including the precise size of her latest passed kidney stone, which she produced in a jar from her coat pocket.

When she finally wheezed to a halt, I found myself in a polite physical and mental paralysis. I tried to find the location of my legs to stand up from my sitting position, but my legs couldn't be found; they had walked away from me 30 minutes earlier, just before her story about the kidney stone entering her bladder. Yet, I learned a lot about my aunt that day by listening to her talk. I learned that her excessive talking was born out of loneliness and out of her fear of death; it was like she wanted to say every word that had ever occurred to her before she died. In addition, her rapid-fire delivery of words filled the room with only her own presence, which gave her a sense of belonging. Overall, her verbosity indicated that she was unsettled spiritually in her heart because her excessive speech gave her the illusion of still being in control.

So, how did I know that my aunt was lonely? She didn't tell me that she was lonely. And how did I know that she needed someone to listen to her to make her feel like she belonged in the world? She didn't tell me it. And how did I know that she was unsettled spiritually in her heart? She didn't talk about it. The answer to these questions lies in the fact that I was not only listening to her words with my ears, but I was also listening to her words with my heart. I was not only using my physical senses to listen; I was also using my spiritual senses to listen and to discern her heart's spiritual condition because she was my mother's 83-year-old sister and because she needed the comfort of someone to talk to. Thus, our conversation was not just taking place through the physical senses of hearing and seeing but on a much higher spiritual plane in the supernatural messaging from the heart. The topics of conversation uttered by her physical voice were not the essence of her message. Those relentless and trivial topics gave way to a much greater spiritual truth. Therefore, two conversations – not one – took place with my aunt on that day. The first conversation was revealed to me by my physical senses and the second conversation was revealed to me by my spiritual senses.

So, a higher form of spiritual communication takes places around us every day that we cannot hear with our ears but can only feel with our heart. Yet, some people go through their entire life hearing Jesus' knock on their heart but never really listen and acknowledge His presence to let Him in. They are too busy physically talking than spiritually listening. If they did listen spiritually to hear Jesus knocking at their heart, they would be the recipient of the food of life; namely, His presence in them that would give their life sustenance and meaning. "… And I will sup with him" (Revelation 3:20) means that Jesus will literally sit down at the table of your spiritual heart and give you the nourishment that you need to feed your soul. When Jesus sits at the table of your heart, He is communing with your soul to give it the nourishment that it needs for you to live a spiritual life. While Jesus waits outside of your heart because of His unanswered knock, you are only living in the world as a physical being. But once you let Jesus into your heart by answering the knock of His supernatural voice, you become a spiritual being now living for Jesus Christ.

Whether you live in Satan's physical world or in the God's spiritual world defines who you are. For instance, Christians live in the Spirit by letting Jesus walk with them in their heart; He is their mentor, guide, and friend. By following His ways set forth in the Bible, they begin to understand the true and deeper spiritual meaning of their life. Therefore, becoming a Christian is a two-way invitation between you and Jesus. It's clear that He wants to be your spiritual dinner guest, but He can't give you that spiritual nourishment if you won't answer and let Him into your heart.

In the physical world, an unexpected knock at the door produces a mystery as to who is on the other side. The sound of the knock automatically gains your attention, and under the circumstance of a mysterious knock, most people in the physical world will answer the door, or at least try to solve the mystery by going over to the door and asking who is there? Wouldn't it be interesting if one morning there was a mysterious knock at the front door of your home and you looked through the door's peep hole to see Jesus standing there? Would you let Him in then? Of course, you would! And right now, He knocks and awaits outside of the door of your heart for your answer. How rude of you not to let in the Guest of Honor

Therefore, being able to hear and understand the Holy Spirit speaking to you through Jesus Christ is the key to your life's transition from living in the physical world to living in the spiritual world. The Holy Spirit is the voice and the feeling that you experience when something is wrong in your life and that it needs fixing. "He that is of God hearth God's words…" (John 8:47). It is the Holy Spirit who will comfort you while this problem is being fixed. As this transition is taking place, you must put more and more faith in God and in His Son Jesus Christ to follow a spiritual path towards healing.

It is essential to understand that Jesus Christ is your guide and mediator with God, and the Holy Spirit is the voice of direct communication from Jesus. Therefore, if you listen to your Holy Spirit, which resides in your soul, you can follow Jesus Christ in life by "feeling" what you should be morally doing according to God. It is a question of doing something right or doing something wrong according to God's Word. Some people would call this "feeling" within them about choosing the right or wrong decision their "conscience." But the term "conscience" is a physical world term and not a spiritual term; hence, the word "conscience" has more of a psychological connotation than a spiritual interpretation. This worldview psychological term refers to the logic of the psyche, and the movement of the spirit is not logical because it cannot be seen, measured, or registered by psychoanalytical means. Therefore, the "feeling" that you have often heard referred to as your conscience is really Jesus talking to you through your Holy Spirit and helping you to choose right from wrong. Without your Holy Spirit silently giving you moral advice and by not being able to "feel" Jesus working in your heart, you would be doomed to follow the immoral, hell bound nonsense of Satan's physical world. So, Jesus Christ gives you a holy option to Satan's bleak forecast for your life. By listening, understanding, and following the Holy Spirit's advice, and by caring about making the morally right decision through Jesus Christ, you can increase your understanding of Jesus' holy authority in you to combat Satan's unholy world and to start distancing yourself from Satan's control. Like many Christians today, you will eventually live in the Spirit of God and be able see life through His holy lens, while still living physically in the perversion of Satan's world. "If ye were of the world, the world would love his own: but because ye are not of the world, but I have chosen you out of the world, therefore the world hateth you" (John 15:8). "But when the Comforter is come, whom I will send unto you from the Father, even the Spirit of truth, which proceedeth from the Father, he shall testify of me: And ye also shall bear witness because ye have been with me from the beginning" (John 26-27).

Living in the spiritual self while living in the physical world is difficult and causes many conflicts. As you can imagine, Satan doesn't like it when your earthly physical self that he controls moves forward into God's spiritual self, and Satan will make your transition from your physical self into your spiritual self very difficult. Remember, Satan temporarily controls the world's systems, so Satan will pull all his earthly levers to get you to return to living only in his physical world.

3. Rethink Money's Importance

"Everybody's been quarreling all day. They're all worried about money." John Cheever, The Enormous Radio

Jesus makes it clear that man cannot serve both God and Satan's money, and when church leaders and religious people place money before God there will be a price to pay. "… It is written, My House shall be called a house of prayer; but ye have made it a den of thieves" (Matthew 21:13). By Jesus tipping over the money changers tables in the Book of Matthew and driving out those religious leaders who took advantage of the people who came to His church to pray, Jesus drew a moral line between doing the good works of the Holy Scripture or taking advantage of them.

In Jesus' time to enter the church at Passover, a person had to bring a sacrifice, such as a dove to offer to God. It was Standard Operating Procedure. According to Leviticus 1:14, "But if his offering to the Lord is a burnt offering of birds, then he shall bring his offering from turtle doves or from young pigeons." However, if someone didn't have a sacrifice, or forgot to bring one, he could buy one before going into church. If you bought a dove to sacrifice while walking into church, Satan was present, and doves were sold at inflated prices, thus gouging churchgoers to make a profit. Just outside the church the prices of doves were often 4 to 10 times higher than the normal price. Hence, Jesus did not like Satan's idea of having to buy your way into church or being rejected from church because you couldn't afford to go. So, if you were selling Satan's sacrifices at inflated prices on that day when Jesus showed up, He showed His displeasure about your greedy actions by driving you away from church. After Jesus' intervention, both the sellers of sacrifices at inflated prices and Satan were driven away from the church property.

In addition to the inflated turtledove prices, the high priests also ordered that the church would only accept Tyrian shekels from churchgoers as a form of money. Tyrian shekels contained a higher percentage of silver. Therefore, when religious pilgrims arrived at the temple during Passover, the money changers demanded to be paid only in Tyrian shekels and then gave back to the pilgrims return coins of lesser value. Satan's unfair monetary exchange rate also angered Jesus, and he drove the money changers from the temple as well because of their greed and thievery. Thus, He calls these money changers "thieves." While the church was established as house of prayer to worship God, in Jesus' time the church leaders and money changers had turned its function into Satan's place of money transaction for profit. This moral line is often crossed even today, as churches ask for money to establish or expand structures and services often unrelated to nurturing faith. Thus, Jesus did not like Satan's influence in the church then and He does not like it now.

When my father grew elderly in his 80's, he decided to sell his fishing boat and motor. Although he and my mother still lived on a lake, he was too frail to launch the boat onto the lake. So, he placed an advertisement in the local township newspaper to sell his boat. My father's ad listed the boat's price at $1,250. A few days later, a middle-aged man showed up at my father's door and wanted to look at the boat, which my dad always kept stored in the garage. My dad was always a stickler about maintaining his mechanical things. The type of equipment didn't matter. Whether shotguns or electric can openers – my father kept it in "tip-top shape." His boat was a prime example of the pride that he placed in his devotion to mechanics. Although the boat was ten-years old, it looked brand new. However, when the middle-aged man decided to buy the boat by producing a roll of cash from his pants pocket, he intentionally misquoted the price of the boat as $1,200 instead of the advertised price of $1,250 and outstretched his hand with the cash. In short, the man was trying to take advantage of an 80-year-old man by short-changing him out of $50 for a boat that was worth much more. My dad looked the man straight in the eye for a long time to let him know that he understood the man's deceit, and then told the man to get off his property.

4. Don't Hide from God; You Can't

"Lord, you have examined me and know all about me. You know when I sit down and when I get up. You know my thoughts before I think them." Psalm 139:1-2

Amos 5:19 addresses the problem Israel will have in escaping the judgement of God for its transgressions. It says that there will be no place to hide in Satan's physical world, even though the people of Israel might think there is a place to hide. In fact, in this verse it states that not only isn't there a place to hide from God, but it is also foolish for anyone to think it. The people of Israel might recognize their sinful ways, but they have not repented from them, and if they did repent, it will be too late. So even if the people of Israel flee from God at the last moment and believe that they can escape His judgement, they are wrong. While temporarily running away from God, Satan might make them believe that they are escaping, but that belief will not last long. For, although they are looking backward and running forward as fast as they can from God for fear of their lives while trying to escape God's punishment by running from a lion, suddenly they run into and meet another deadly predator—a bear. The irony is, of course, that you cannot outrun God and win the race. Because just as soon as you believe that you have outrun God's judgement, then another catastrophe will befall you. Therefore, while Satan might make the people of Israel and people today think by their sinful behavior and by not repenting from it that they are smarter and swifter afoot than God, they are not.

Furthermore, even though you think that you have won the footrace with God, even though you have not repented from your sins, and even though you might breathe a sigh of relief when you reach the safety of your own house after a fast and long run, God will still reach into your house to find you. He will still have catastrophe befall you because you are not repentant of your sinful ways. In this case, the unrepentant sinner is exhausted after running with Satan from God, arrives at his house, closes and locks the door, and then leans on the wall in exhaustion only to be bitten by a poisonous snake. In short, you need to understand that there is nowhere to run and nowhere to hide from God, and the sooner you know this and become obedient to Him and repent from your sin and live in the Spirit—the better off you will be. Shakespeare said it best in King Henry the Eighth, "We may outrun by violent swiftness. And lose by over-running."

5. Acknowledge the Sin within You

"No man knows how bad he is till he has tried very hard to be good."
—CS Lewis, Mere Christianity

When Philip went to Samaria to teach the Word of Jesus in Acts 8:9-24, he encountered many psychologically and physically stricken people, whom he healed. At the time, the early Christian church seemed to be in disarray, yet in Samaria the people seemed to be of one accord and accepted Jesus. However, in Samaria there was a man named Simon, who was a sorcerer and bewitched people. Evidently, Simon's incantations were taken seriously by many people; some people even thought he was from God. At first, Simon opposed Philip's teachings about Christ, probably because Simon had his own deceived followers and didn't want to relinquish them to Philip to follow Christ. Then, Simon "believed also: and when he was baptized, he continued with Philip" (Acts 8:13). So, it appears that Simon had a change of heart about Jesus Christ and threw his support to the apostle and was baptized. However, this would have been a great conversion-to-Christ story in the early church. Namely, someone who had at one time had been opposed to Jesus, and had once been a satanic sorcerer himself, saw the light through the miracles performed by Philip and came to Christ. Unfortunately, for Simon the story does not end here; Satan intervened and Simon's fate of becoming a true convert to Christ flounders. After Simon—with Satan in him—follows Philip, Simon soon marvels about Philip's ability to perform miracles by healing the possessed and the lame, and Simon experiences Satan's influence again by watching something being delivered by Philip that harkens back Simon's old incantation ways. Simon sees Peter and John laying their hands-on people so that they could receive the Holy Ghost, and Simon wants this ability too. Of course, he is not one of the original apostles to which Jesus gave this power, so no matter how much Satan and Simon want this power, they aren't going to receive it. This is something Simon apparently cannot accept so with Satan now full blown in his heart he offered the apostles money to teach him how to impart the Holy Spirit. Peter knows that Simon's attempt to bribe him with money to get the power to import the Holy Spirit is Satan's work. In fact, Peter says to Simon "… thy money perish with thee, because thou hast thought that the gift of God may be purchased with money" (Acts 8:20).

So, it appears that Simon's thought process had not, after all, left the satanic incantation stage. Simon probably made good money fooling people with his sorcery; he probably even made some people believe that Satan's false hope was real, and despite his profession of faith and his dutifully following and watching the apostles heal people from the hand of God, Simon still thinks that the imparting of the Holy Spirit was still within the realm of Satan's secular magic and he was willing to pay money to receive it. It must have been disheartening to the Apostles who had experienced Simon's conversion to Christ and then evidenced Satan's return in him. In fact, in Acts 8:21-22, Peter rebukes Simon for relying on money instead of on God. "Thou hast neither part nor lot in this matter: for thy heart is not right in the sight of God. Repent therefore of this thy wickedness, and pray God, if perhaps the thought of thine heart may be forgiven thee." So, ultimately it seems that Simon comes to realize his mistake and asks for the Apostles to pray for him in order for him to reject Satan. The first step for any person—Christian or not—is to understand their sin and that they need Jesus Christ as their Savior for redemption. Then, they need to ask for His forgiveness. In short, this story is a microcosm of every person's will to reject Satan and to receive a Christian conversion to Christ and the struggle against sin still within them.

6. Live Moderately

"You must confine yourself within the modest limits of order." Shakespeare, Twelfth Night

Paul in 1 Corinthians 9:25 speaks to every Christian's understanding and adherence to moderation in all things in life if they are to gain the Kingdom of God. "And every man that striveth for the mastery is temperate in all things" (Corinthians 9:25). If you think about it, most people get into trouble because of their excessiveness. It is alright to indulge in worldly things if those indulgences are not sinful and do not become excessive and create Satan's stumbling block to knowing Jesus.

However, people in the United States have a difficult time practicing moderate behavior; Satan's influence in the United States presents a culture that promotes excessive behavior. For example, if you compare the food portions served on a plate to a customer at a restaurant in the US to the food portions served on a plate at a restaurant in other countries, the US food portions served on a plate are two or three times larger than the food portions plated in other countries. The mealtime expectation in the US is that more food is better and that too much food is even better. Look at the number of US restaurants that serve all-you-can-eat buffets, and then look at the size of the patrons who regularly eat at them.

This United States mealtime excess is just the opposite of what Paul states in 1 Corinthians 9:25; Christians should be temperate in all things. Why should Christians be temperate? Because moderation demonstrates Christian self-control, and self-control demonstrates a Christian lifestyle that places the Lord Jesus first. Christians should love Jesus more than a hot fudge sundae, and by denying themselves a hot fudge sundae that they don't need for dessert, Christians reject Satan's excess and demonstrate a self-controlled behavior that is more becoming to Jesus. "Let your moderation be known unto all men. The Lord is at hand" (Philippians 4:5).

When Jesus sent His disciples forth into the world to preach the gospel, He did not send them forth with a wagon train caravan of food stuffs for their journey. He did not weight His disciples down with carrying a 100-pound side of beef. In fact, Jesus sent his disciples forth into the world without any food because the Lord will provide and because it demonstrated His priorities of importance. Jesus comes first before any worldly thing. Therefore, a Christian who does not control himself and does not practice moderation in all things in life is simply tempting Satan and not practicing a Christian lifestyle. By not curtailing his appetite for worldly things, he is demonstrating that sometimes Christ is not placed first in his life, and this often leads to Christ-first only on Sunday behavior. The ancient Greeks espoused the same moderate lifestyle approach as Paul. The ancient Greeks called for living a moderate lifestyle by following "The Golden Mean," which meant nothing to excess by staying in the middle. Today, just like for the ancient Greeks and for Paul in 1 Corinthians 9:25, nothing good comes from excess because Satan's excess breeds more excess—no matter the endeavor. And the more excessive a Christian becomes, the more important those excesses become to him, until eventually Satan replaces the only excess allowed in this world—a Christian's love for Jesus Christ.

7.   Listen to the Holy Spirit—Jesus' Messenger

"All ministries, therefore, must be subjected to this test—if they do not glorify Christ, they are not of the Holy Spirit."

—Charles Spurgeon, The Holy Spirit's Chief Office

Years ago, while an undergraduate student, I went snowshoeing in

Michigan's Upper Peninsula. The UP of Michigan receives hundreds of inches of snow per year. Usually, the winters are long and mean, which makes it even more imperative to brave the winter weather and to get outside to avoid cabin fever. The year that I avoided cabin fever, the gunpower skies had dropped close to two hundred inches of snow, and in some places—like in the deep woods where I went snowshoeing—the snow had drifted to a seven or eight feet depth. The seven to eight feet snow depth was something that I didn't become aware of until I had accidently fallen into it. At the time of my fall, I was 45 minutes back into the deep woods and enjoying the winter's fresh smell of the pine trees, when I suddenly spotted a porcupine sitting in a low hanging branch of a dead pine tree. I first saw the porcupine out of the corner of my right eye, and then I turned to confirm what I saw. When I suddenly turned to get a better look, I lost my balance and fell sideways down into the deep snow. In a flash, I knew that I was in trouble. While before I had been safely walking atop the seven feet of snow on my snowshoes, after my fall I was now looking up at the blue sky buried deep in it. At first, I tried to thrash my way out of my snowy ravine by flailing my arms about to get back on top of the snow's surface. Then, I realized that I wouldn't be able to simply climb out of my depth, but I had to slowly and painstakingly "trudge" my way out, gradually climbing out of my snowy cavern one foot at a time by building a ledge.

It took me about one-quarter of a mile to slowly build a ledge with my snowshoes to eventually climb out of my snowy tomb, and that's the same way it is for many people who suddenly find themselves in too deep in the circumstances of life. For them, there isn't a quick fix either to solve the depth of their problem because the sudden fall has taken them a long time to get into the mess, and now it will take a long time to get out of it. This is when listening to the voice of Jesus through the Holy Spirit for guidance makes all the difference in the world. Having Jesus by your side to solve life's problems will help you to understand that you are a sinner and in need of His help. When I fell into the deep snow on that winter's day while snowshoeing deep into the Northern Michigan woods, the temperature was at minus 10 degrees below zero. Immediately, I prayed to Jesus to save me. I could have easily frozen to death out there in the middle of the pointless forest, and my body probably wouldn't have been found, if ever, until the spring snow melt. On that day, the Lord Jesus was with me, and the quiet and calming voice of the Holy Spirit directed me on how to exit the snowy tomb and how to make my way safely back to the warmth of the log cabin. That snowshoeing incident took place over fifty years ago, and I haven't been snowshoeing since, not even in two inches of snow. I learned a valuable lesson about not taking unnecessary risks with my life and about my dependence on Jesus and His Holy Spirit for safety and comfort.

The Book of Ephesians instructs Christians to understand and to be ready to do battle with Satan by putting on the armour of God. "Put on the whole armour of God, that ye may be able to stand against the wiles of the devil" (Ephesians 6:11). The whole armour of God includes making good moral decisions by consulting with the Holy Spirit. A Christian's defense against the darkness of the world is in shining God's light into its dark places. By reading God's Word in the Bible, which Ephesians calls the "sword of the Spirit" (Ephesians 6:17), praying, and listening to the Holy Spirit within you, God will give you the understanding to navigate through this evil world with Christian confidence by illuminating the goodness of your soul by praying to the Holy Spirit to shine forth God's direction for you by exposing the dark temptations of Satan, and thereby nourishing your spiritual self and becoming closer and stronger in Jesus.

8. Remember: Your Salvation Starts Today

"As a well spent day brings happy sleep, so life well used brings happy death." Leonardo da Vinci, The Notebooks

In 2 Corinthians 6, Paul asks the people of Corinth not to receive "… the grace of God in vain." That is, you should understand that God doesn't want you to take your salvation lightly, lest you backslide to your old and former self. He said also that "… now is the accepted time, behold, now is the day of salvation" (2 Corinthians 6:2). Therefore, not only is it important, but God wants you to understand that there is also no time to waste and none to spare because "We then, as workers together with Him, beseech you…" (2 Corinthians 6:1). So, Paul is imploring the people of Corinth to receive the grace of God (salvation), to receive it now, and not to take the receiving of it lightly because Paul and others, as fellow workers for Christ, have brought the people of Corinth to the edge of commitment to Christ, and now—through Christ—they must take the next step forward to receive Him.

By doing so, however, they must understand that God expects their hearts to be in the right place because if it is, then they will also become partakers in the mysterious glory found in Christ, a glory that often seems odd and unrealistic to others who live outside of Christ's salvation in Satan's fallen world. However, by knowing that they have entered into a bond with Jesus Christ through their salvation, they will know the truth about the secular world where Satan temporally reigns.

In knowing the truth about the secular world through their salvation, they come to see Satan's world realistically as fallen and without hope, unless people embrace salvation's hope given by Christ. Furthermore, a newly saved Christian will start to see the stark differences in perspective between Christian values and Satan's secular values in a fallen world. In short, while the world believes this; the Christian will believe that. Thus, in 2 Corinthians 6:10, Paul states, "As sorrowful, yet always rejoicing; as poor, yet making many rich; as having nothing, and yet possessing all things."

So, God expects a Christian's lifestyle and beliefs to be different from a secular world's lifestyle and beliefs. While a Christian may appear to be sorrowful to a secular person, he is sorrowful for those who don't yet know Christ and he rejoices in his own salvation through Christ. And while many people in the secular world will perceive a Christian as poor because of his lack of material possessions, the Christian sees himself as rich because he has—through his salvation—been given the most valuable gift in one's life. Therefore, while many secular people will contend that Christians are poor and unhappy, Christians are just the opposite because they possess all spiritual truth through their salvation in Jesus Christ.

Furthermore, no one knows the end time of the world; Christians call it The Great Tribulation. Therefore, no one should delay in coming to the Lord because there not be a tomorrow. "But of that day and that hour knoweth no man, no, not the angels which are in heaven, neither the Son, but the Father. Take ye heed, watch and pray: for ye know not when the time is" (Mark 13:32-33).

The difference in personal viewpoints between a saved Christian and a secular person is the difference between vision during the day and vision at night. A Christian always walks in the light of Christ, which illuminates his way by helping him to make good moral decisions.

Christ's light also shines ahead of a Christian because the Holy Spirit is his inner moral compass; it is the voice of Christ in him. "Thy word is a lamp unto my feet, and a light unto my path" (Psalm 119:105). Thus, a Christian's constant companion is Jesus Christ. By contrast, a secular man's companion is Satan in himself. He makes his decisions by himself with Satan whispering in his ear; and whether those decisions are moral doesn't matter. A secular man's decisions are made with a short-sighted vision, like one stumbling while walking in the dark. "And a stone of stumbling, and a rock of offence, even to them which stumble at the word, being disobedient…." (1 Peter 2:8). When a non-believer's stumbling causes him to lose his balance, he grabs onto anything in this world to try to keep him from falling. Eventually, however, he will find that nothing in Satan's world will support him long enough to keep him from falling because nothing except Jesus Christ's salvation can do that.

9. Know Your Spiritual Ancestry

"Teach that God is, not was; that He speaketh, not spake." Ralph Waldo Emerson, Journals and Miscellaneous Notebooks

I love 2 Corinthians 3:3 because it tells all Christians that they are the living and breathing spiritual descendants of Jesus Christ. Because Christians are the living testimony of Christ's mission on earth, the historical and spiritual significance of His life lives on in us; it is, in fact, a legacy passed on to the living, and not one contained in the dead and in ancient manuscripts and tablets of stone. "Forasmuch as ye are manifestly declared to be the epistle of Christ ministered by us, written not with ink but with the Spirit of the living God; not in tables of stone, but in fleshy tables of the heart" (2 Corinthians 3:3). Therefore, Christ's gift of salvation and our receipt of it are as alive today as it was when Christ walked the earth. And because Christ is in us through His Holy Spirit, we are the living record of Him today. By our Christian actions and values, we reflect who Christ was and is and why He was sent by God to earth. We are His children living in the world today as a testament to His life because we know that He was sent by God to save our souls. His gift of salvation allows a Christian the ability to be both human and mortal, yet to live spiritually and immortal. The actions related to this condition and what God expects of us continues the undying and eternal narrative of Christ's life on earth. By spreading His

Good News in Satan's fallen world, we become Jesus' contemporary disciples. Thus, His mission of salvation continues today through every Christian.

By Christians believing in the message of Christ, they become the embodiment of His spirit, and Christ comes alive once again today through them. Through them, the Bible's ink of the Old and New Testaments is lifted from the parchment page and tablets of stone and into the hearts of people. Every time a Christian's prayer carries on their desire to do the work of Jesus because it is written in their heart, the Holy Spirit moves them along the path towards bringing other people to Christ and someday being reunited with Him. Those living Christian movements and moments of prayer spell the letters and words of the Bible in the hearts of others. Therefore, Jesus is more than just inked words on a page, and more than just an official law of stone; the Word of Jesus takes living root in people's souls and grows them into Christians who reflect the value of Christ's life. Indeed, even non-believers can recognize Jesus in the world today because His spirit moves by His command in us. He calls all His own to Him to perform His Christian functions; we are the living book of Christ. And, through our actions we help extend with Christ's sanction the gift of salvation to others. "The Lord is my light and my salvation; whom shall I fear? The Lord is the strength of my life; of whom shall I be afraid?" (Psalm 27:1).

Therefore, Christ lives on earth today through and in a Christian. Because of Christ's living in them and His gift of salvation to them, Christians have learned to live from a spiritual place in their heart, where Christ's Holy Spirit lives. The Bible is certainly something to read and know, but it is equally important to feel the Word of Christ working and tugging at your heart. Once a person feels Christ's eternal residence in their heart, then they have become His Word lifted off the Bible's page and set into motion in the world. And it is this Christian movement reflecting Christ's message in the world by living in the spiritual heart-side out that extends Christ presence in the world from generation to generation and from cradle to grave.

10. Guard Against Sinful Distractions

"Great men are they who see that spiritual is stronger than material force." – Ralph Waldo Emerson

If you think about it, Satan's physical world is very loud. External noise suppresses your ability to think by distracting your attention. Satan puts evil thoughts in your mind, yet it is your spiritual job to combat them. Remember, the battle for your soul is a moment-by-moment confrontation. Evil thoughts like impulse buying is a great example of Satan's distractive and disruptive power. In impulsive buying, the shopper had no intention of buying what they bought, that is, until they saw it and were convinced to buy it by its psychological and emotional allure. For instance, jewelry store owners often display their merchandise under gleaming bright lights on black velvet in a mirrored showcase, which makes the items sparkle and suggest exclusivity. Thus, the item's marketing presentation creates a sense of glamour and urgency. Here, however, Satan is at work in controlling your shopping habits and your emotional response to buy an item. Satan knows that you already own three of these items, yet he just wants to see if he can push enough of your emotional buttons to get you to buy another one. What matters is that Satan has just invaded into your thoughts to convince you to buy something that you don't need. Warriors for Christ, this is an example of how commercial interests influence the battle for your soul every day on earth. Every day you are faced with decisions that influence what to buy and who is winning the battle for our soul, and both God or Satan are at work while watching you and what's going on in every moment of your life. They watch as your soul tips towards hell with a bad decision and then comes back to tip towards heaven with a good decision. And then, your soul tips towards hell again, and so forth, as one power gains the advantage for your soul at the moment over the other.

For example, when I was eight years of age, I saw my first motor scooter. It was on a stairway landing leading to the basement of the Sears toy department. The scooter was bright red, and it had a price of $325 on the windshield. To this day, I haven't forgotten the gleaming appeal of owning that motor scooter. Now and then, I still think about it. Yet, now the argument about buying one is less about the price of the scooter and more about my safety while riding it. Yet why does that one motor scooter seen sixty years ago still linger in my memory? Why can I still see it so vividly in my mind today? The answer to these questions resides in Satan's relentless pursuit for your soul. Sixty years later, my mind's eye can see that motor scooter just like I was seeing it for the first time. This is how Satan extends his pursuit for our soul throughout a lifetime by planting re-occurring memories about frivolous things that we desire but don't need.

Another re-occurring memory as an 8-year-old child started when I saw my first Chris-Craft Boat. I was on a two-week summer vacation with my parents who had rented a cottage at Devil's Lake. (No kidding that was the name of the lake.) The wooden inboard Chris-Craft Boat was owned by a young man who had prospered by owning a gravel pit. I had previously seen the Dale's Cement trucks on the highways, so not only did he have his name on a multitude of cement trucks, but he also owned the Chris-Craft beauty—the most precious boat on the lake. Some guys have all the breaks, and his ego knew that he had been fortunate in life. You could tell it by the way he raced his boat up and down the length of the lake at full throttle, inching it up to 55 mile per hour just to back the engine down to listen to the exhaust pipes babble in a deep mellow purr. It was a pretty sound to be sure, one that would send any garage mechanic to church to sign up for the church choir. Yes, it was a boat to see. Its polished wood was varnished to perfection with a gleam that gathered sunlight together in an angelic fashion. Once, I walked onto his dock to look at the boat's interior. I wasn't supposed to be on the man's dock, but for some reason I just had to look at the inside of the boat—no matter the costs. The boat's red leather seats were curved and fitted flawlessly into the rounded wood seats so that the passengers rode snug in the boat's interior like astronauts strapped into a space capsule. The moment that I saw that Chris-Craft boat, I too aspired to be a gravel pit owner. At the time, I'd do anything just to have a boat like that. And now, of course, the Chris-Craft classic 1960's models are so expensive that you'd have be a Bellwether family member just to own one. Yet, even now sixty years later while I live on a bluff overlooking the Mississippi River, where great barges float lazily passed every day, I still stretch my neck and scan the water's horizon in the off-chance that I might still catch a glimpse of one. And this is how Satan works desire and envy in the hearts of people to make them covet things instead of God.

Therefore, Satan's evil work takes place over a lifetime, and he'll test you from an early age to discover your vulnerabilities. For me, I like to look at motor scooters and boats. Someone else might like to look at cars and women. Whatever your vulnerability, Satan will try to find it and to exploit it against you to lead you down a path away from God. Sometimes it is a life-long battle against Satan because he has found your weakness early in life. If your weakness is women, he will make the encounter happen for you to meet one to test your resolve, then he will watch and await your decision. If your vulnerability is drugs, then you can expect Satan will have you meet users and suppliers to test your ability to say no. You get the point: Satan will find your weakness and exploit it to his advantage and to your detriment. He is a master at deception and disguise to make you believe things that are untrue. Just look at how advertising manipulates people by romanticizing items as unique and special, although buying the item will not make you also unique and special as suggested. In my case with the motor scooter and the Chris-Craft boat, Satan has taken up a life-long, jealous residence in my mind by providing me with distant longings, jealousy, and memories about things I admired but could never own. His goal is to create a desire for the use of the items to manipulate my thoughts against my Holy Spirit. Remember, it is not only the item that Satan wants you think about. The item is not his primary goal; it is only a conduit. His primary goal is to use the item(s) to manipulate your thoughts away from God by fantasizing about something else. In truth, the only acceptable excessive behavior is the one directed toward knowing Jesus Christ.

In this regard, prayer is a powerful force for good, and praying to Jesus often and regularly about everyday decisions and who is directing them is a good thing to do. Satan is a wily serpent, and he has created a dangerous world full of minefields of deceit and deception. Only one thing is for sure in Satan's world: what you see isn't what you get. This is one reason why the world is becoming more and more complex by the complications presented by ordinary things in our everyday lives. It might sound crazy, but I believe that Satan loves to burn time off your life by forcing you to concentrate on unnecessary technological items. Much of technology is not worth the time spent on learning how to use it. For instance, to change the television channel when I was a boy, I simply walked to the tv set and turn the dial. Today, however, many people spend an extraordinary amount of time learning about how to operate complicated technological gadgets like a tv remote control because Satan deceives them into thinking that because they can now use it that they are somehow smarter, when just the opposite is happening. By expending the additional time necessary to perform a simple task because of added complications, you have burdened yourself with another unnecessary and time-consuming task. Once you accept these additional complications as normal advancements, then you have opened the door for Satan to make your life increasingly more complicated and stressful. The more time that you spend figuring out how Satan's smokescreen of technological interference works, the less time you can devote to the development of your spiritual self. By burning hours off your life by concentrating on learning needless technology, Satan distracts you from thinking about more important matters –like examining life and its consequences for the eternal destination for your soul.

Satan's world believes that more complication is good. When, in fact, less complicated is good. If the same goal can be accomplished faster, simpler, and easier, than how can more complex and time-consuming technologies be better? Therefore, Satan is running out the clock on our lives by having us indulge in trivial technological gadgets rather that thinking about the larger spiritual questions before us. In fact, many Christians live a simple lifestyle so that they can focus their attention on their relationship with Jesus Christ by keeping uninvited technological complications to a minimum. They see the world realistically as a domain temporary controlled by Satan where no one can truly find peace. My point is simply this: the complication of more and more time-consuming gadgets in life won't help you to find the loving grace of our Lord Jesus Christ. In fact, technology often hinders us and blinds us from pursuing more important spiritual matters. To seek the love of Jesus Christ, you must jettison the worldly elements that interfere and unnecessarily complicate and compete for your time and that prevent you from seeking Him by praying and reading the Bible. Any activity that does not reward you by growing spiritually should be examined as to whether it is necessary or important. Remember, Satan wants you to believe that he knows what's best for you. But if you pray to Jesus for direction about whether your behavior concerning an item is good or bad, then you will get an honest answer. Satan, of course, will not give you an honest answer because if he does it will diminish his control over you.

If you pray and listen to your Holy Spirit, you will begin to exercise Christian self-restraint against the purchase and use of many unnecessary items and to understand that possessions on earth have no value in heaven; they are only served up by Satan to occupy your mind and time on earth. Therefore, while shopping you are given a moral imperative that indicates whether you're living in the physical self or in the spiritual self. Every decision asks you to make a moral choice, and the wrong choice promotes Satan's agenda and limits your time with Jesus.

If the battle for your soul is taking place between God and Satan on every decision you make in the physical world, then you must know what God expects of you in order to make the correct decision. In the previous examples, we saw that Satan promotes excessive time devoted to technology and consumerism and that God through the Holy Spirit does not like it. However, how do you know what God likes and dislikes as it relates to your consumer behavior? The only way to know God's preference and what he expects of you is by reading the Bible. The Bible is The Instruction Manual for Life, and it essential in discerning what God, the Father; His Son Jesus Christ, and the Holy Spirit wants you to do in life. The Bible gives people the necessary instructions for living a spiritual life by giving spiritual beings their direction about how to live and survive morally on Satan's earth. Without the spiritual instruction found in the Bible, people wouldn't know how God wants them to live. Therefore, reading the Bible for spiritual instruction and direction is essential for growing more spiritual and knowing how to live as a Christian. "All scripture is given by inspiration of God, and is profitable for doctrine, for reproof, for correction, for instruction in righteousness" (2 Timothy 3:16).

11. Control Your Ego

"No act is so private it does not seek applause." John Updike, Couples

Matthew 13:22 states "… the deceitfulness of riches, choke the word.…" And nothing is more offensive than seeing people who think that they are better than other people. For if they think they are better, they are woefully wrong. Everyone is born of the same hand of God, and everyone will also die of the same hand of God. Death does not discriminate. So, if everyone eventually ends up in the same circumstance of dying, it ultimately means that we—because of that similar and singular end—are indeed all equal. But this collective fate is not often entered into the calculation of the selfish, who believe that their life for Satan's superficial reasons is more important than other's. This, however, is a false premise based on a combination of fear and theatrics.

Anyone who walks around with their ego as a best friend is afraid of being exposed for who and what they are—no better than anybody else. It is this fear of being ordinary that prompts them to act like they are not. Instead of owning up to the fact that they, too, are simply deteriorating human flesh from the day of their birth until the day of their death, they use theatrical props to make themselves appear more worldly important. This, of course, is only Satan's superficial display of idol worship—of placing their love and use of things before their love of God. If God wanted us to place the value of ourselves on what kind of car we drive, we would have been born with 16" Goodyear radial tires instead of feet. And if God placed any value on the clothes we wear, we would all be born wearing James Bond tuxedoes. The fact that we are all born naked, afraid, and dependent on God makes this world all clear: All human beings are born equal and no earthly trinket of Satan can alter it. We are born, we live, and we die. This is how God works it for everyone. To not understand that we are all equal in God's eyes is a dangerous proposition. For, if we put our faith in the inequality of humans based on the trinkets of Satan, then we have bought into Satan's version of life which says that we are all inherently unequal based upon how many things we own.

I once knew a person who could not share even with his own family because of his ego. In everything in life, he had to buy the best for himself and had to be served first before anyone in his family. One time, he was sent to pick up a pizza for his family at a local pizza parlor, and upon his return home when his family opened up the pizza box to serve themselves they discovered that the two largest pizza pieces were missing. On the drive home from the pizza parlor, the egoist had opened the pizza box and had taken out and eaten the biggest two pizza slices himself. The fact that he was stealing the pieces from his own wife and his two children didn't concern him; he wanted to get served first and with the biggest pizza slices because his ego told him that he was more important than them.

It is Satan's work in the world that perpetually tries to prove that inequality based on money, possessions, and power is inevitable and that it is the scale that weighs a person's self-worth. This satanic calculation of self-worth eliminates the very equal essence of our birth by God; that is, we are all born, and we will all die. God is an equal opportunity employer. He hired us on earth when we were born, and He will fire us on earth when we die, and nothing except following His commandments makes much difference in-between. So, the high-and-mighty Pharisees in Jesus' time, if they were alive today, would have probably driven Cadillacs or Mercedes, would have probably resided in Malibu or vacationed on the French Riviera, and would have probably worn Gucci this or Gucci that. But even with their spit-shined egos, they too would still experience death and their souls would still hold a reckoning with God. "For if ye live after the flesh, ye shall die: but if ye through the Spirit do mortify the deeds of the body, ye shall live" (Romans 8:13).

So, not much has changed since the church-ruling Pharisees' egos got the best of them 2,000 years ago, except maybe the box seat tickets have moved from the synagogue to the Kennedy Center. Egos are still egos, and Satan's self-delusion is still self-delusion. Only through listening to the quiet voice of the Holy Spirit within us—when God speaks to us in our emptiness—can we really begin to understand the humanness of our equality in God's eyes and weigh-in on the scales of what it means to be a human being under His authority. "For I say, through the grace given unto me, to every man that is among you, not to think of himself more highly than he ought to think; but to think soberly, according as God hath dealt to every man the measure of faith" (Romans 12:3). Despite Satan's economic disparity and influence in the world, the only notable inequality in people's lives worthy of mention is the amount of their personal investment of time they have made in their relationship with Jesus Christ. Satan has established materialism as window-dressing for inequality, but at the end of each life the equality of death awaits, and God always has the last word.

12. Remember: You're a Child of God

"The child of God works not for life, but from life; he does not work to be saved but works because he is saved." —Charles Spurgeon

Children in our society are often ignored because adults believe that children have nothing worthwhile to say. After all, they don't have enough of life's experiences on which to draw to make a rational decision, and they are completely reliant on others for their care and well-being. Yet, Jesus in Luke 18:17 says this about children. "Verily I say until you, whosoever shall not receive the kingdom of God as a little child shall in no wise enter therein." Therefore, in this verse Jesus exults a child to a heavenly level by stating that everyone must become a child again to enter heaven. Therefore, despite what the world says about the inexperience of children, they must have some redeeming qualities for Jesus to place them first in line to get to heaven. Therefore, what child-like attributes make being a child so valuable to Jesus and spiritual life?

First, a child is innocent and totally reliant on someone else, just like everyone should be reliant on Jesus. Children have not yet learned the ways of a fallen world—ways that are the paths of Satan. Therefore, adults should not assume that the deceitful ways of the world and winning worldly competitions are necessarily good things. For instance, a child does not masquerade as someone else—like so many adults who assume different personas throughout the day to fit a role to play to a specific audience. Adults change their diction, dress, and demeanor to fit the occasion and audience. A child speaks, acts, and will wear the same clothes day after day for everyone. In short, a child doesn't care about the social conventions of this world and whether they might prove acceptable or economically profitable. Therefore, children live outside the socially acceptable norm, and their actions, appearance, and speech are often outside this world's acceptance because they have yet to conform to the ways of a fallen world. This is what Jesus alludes to when he elevates a child's innocence above knowing and using the conventions of a fallen world. "Suffer little children, and forbid them not, to come unto me: for of such is the kingdom of heaven" (Matthew 10:14).

Because a child is still trusting and pure, he is more likely to hear and pursue a path to Jesus than an adult who has been polluted in action and thought by the influence of Satan. Exulting an innocent child to be eligible to enter heaven before everyone else is so like Jesus' philosophy of "But many that are first shall be last; and the last shall be first" (Matthew 19:30). Whoever a fallen world thinks should be going to heaven first probably won't get there, and the person who the fallen world thinks won't get to heaven probably will. This juxtaposed perspective is especially true for adults when they proclaim their good works as their leverage with God to get into heaven. After all, a child's short life doesn't contain the good works that an adult has accomplished. An adult's good works throughout life will certainly out weigh the absence of good works from a child to tip the moral scales to get into heaven. Yet, this is precisely the type of satanic thinking in a fallen world that Jesus addresses to be false.

Fortunately, for me many of my childhood personality traits have not been extinguished by the adult world while growing up. I thank God for the perseverance of my childhood imagination throughout my life. Even at the age of 72, I still love the magic of words and the creation of story invention. Many things in the adult world have been disappointing to me, and I believe that that disappointment stems from the fact that I still live as a child in an adult body. That's why it is easy for me to see and feel the injustice in the world and discern dishonest personalities in it. The gift of adult discernment from a childhood perspective has always been one of my strongest personality traits, and God's gift of it to me has served me well. And most of this discernment stems from still viewing the world from the eyes of a child. Because the world seldom pays attention to anyone who isn't productive in the economy—like the elderly and young people—when you say something interesting with a "turn of phrase" as an adult from a child's perspective, it is often perceived as unique and inventive, although from a child's perspective, it is just another day of living and talking as a child. The difference is about still seeing the world from a child-like perspective, which sparks the inventiveness of language and imagination. In short, still being a child as an adult often liberates the creative nature in people.

For instance, as a child I played the card game of Crazy Eights with five other imaginary players. I'd deal the cards out around the kitchen table to the other invisible players, imagined what the other players looked like, and then talked to them as the game progressed. I was playing this card game at the kitchen table one evening when my father stopped and asked me what I was doing. I described the appearance of the other players to him and then resumed my card game with them by speaking to an invisible player at the far end of the table. "You talk to them too?" my father asked. "Of course," I replied. My father then left immediately for the living room where I heard him ask my mother, "Do you know that Stephen is playing cards with five imaginary players that he talks to?" My mother, who was a musician and artist, answered "Yes, Isn't it wonderful!"

Later in life, those five imaginary Crazy Eight players appeared as characters in my first novel, The Last Chord Concert, which is an imaginary tale about rock and roll music in the 45th Century and music played by the band The Rocket Launchers in gigs in space lounges light years away. As you can see, you can still be creative at any age if you still live somewhat apart from your adultness and in the inquisitive nature of a child.

Unfortunately, many adults have been contaminated as adults by the lure of Satan's fallen world; the influences of Satan have disturbed their adult's sense of child-like spiritual proportion. In fact, as Jesus points out, it is precisely a child's innocent lack of worldly experience that qualifies him/her first to enter into heaven. A child's lack of Satan's worldly experience is a plus, and it is something that all adults should acquire again. If an adult—after experiencing the influences of Satan in the world—can still maintain the innocence of heart and a child's faithful obedience and dependence on Jesus to take care of him/her, then an adult can rightfully proclaim that their faith and God's grace—and not their worldly accomplishments—have gotten him into Christendom. Like a child, we are all dependent on God's help for our life and the sustaining of it. When an adult reaches the conclusion that God—and not Satan—decides on whether he gets the next breath of air, then he can genuinely say that he has once again become a child of God. In this vain, I once read an article that stated that only 2% to 3% of people over the age of 30 years accept salvation from Jesus. Perhaps the reason for this low percentage of people over the age of 30 being saved is because their childhood innocence and dependence has become polluted by Satan's deceit found in the adult world.

13. Live a Spirit-Filled Life

"I believe this is one of the tests of the Spirit-filled life. Is Christ becoming more and more evident in my life? Are people seeing more of Him, and less of Me?" —Billy Graham

To enter the Kingdom of God and not be turned away, you must first follow a strait path in life according to the teachings of Jesus Christ. "Strive to enter in at the strait gate: for many, I say unto you, will seek to enter in, and shall not be able" (Luke 13:24). A strait life's path means not diverting from the life's path provided for you by God's Word in the Bible. The Bible is the Instruction Manual for Life, and to follow a strait path that leads to the strait gate to heaven, a Christian must be consciously diligent to live a life according to the precepts and conditions stated in the Bible. By not varying or straying off the path of God's Word, the Christian can live a moral life and then enter into God's Kingdom.

However, while many people read the Bible, many people still fall short of entering through the strait gate because they are not consciously living a life that guards against the wiles of Satan. Satan's only world assignment is to alter your walk with God. If Satan can make you believe that you are the center of your own universe by tempting you with immoral choices, then he has a good chance of making you stray from the strait path that leads to the straight gate of heaven. Many of Satan's ways can influence a weak Christian; that is, one who takes his Christian faith lightly. Furthermore, Satan can also influence people's moral path because of incorrect church doctrine that diverts people away from adherence to the Bible's scripture.

For instance, some church doctrines clearly espouse principles that are contrary to the Bible's scripture and are injurious to people's spiritual health. Take works, for instance. Many people by following the doctrine espoused by their religion are trying by their own good works to work their way into heaven. To them, the more good works they do on earth; the greater their chances of going to heaven. This is Satan's deceit. Nothing could be further from the truth. You can do nothing by yourselves to work or earn your way into heaven. Your entry into heaven is given to you; it is a gift from God. Yes, it is a gift from God that will determine whether you are saved and can go to heaven. "For by grace are ye saved through faith and that not of yourselves: it is the gift of God: Not of works, lest any man should boast" (Ephesians 2:8-9). A faith-filled Christian, however, should do good works because they are a Christian, but while good works might identify a Christian, it does not define him and qualify him for heavenly housing; only God can do that!

Therefore, is it possible for some people to be deceived by Satan into thinking that a lifetime of good works will lead to heavenly real estate? Absolutely! That is why some people are very surprised when they "…

seek to enter in and shall not be able" (*Luke 13:24*). *Seek* is an interesting word choice used by Jesus. People who rely on themselves to seek (i.e., search) for a way to get heaven will be turned away. Seeking it by your own efforts will fail because in the end it is God's house, and He determines who gets to live there.

I once lived in a conceited religious community where I could feel the self-righteousness of the people who lived there because they thought that they had secured the only pathway to heaven. The church taught doctrines that exclusively made them the sole heirs to get to heaven. Therefore, their smugness and arrogance about their sole heavenly-bound status could be felt and seen in everyday life. Physically, they walked with their nose in the air with an arrogance that can only come from ignorance, and their ego had become so inflated that they only talked to and did business with people of like religious belief. Therefore, in this community, if you didn't attend a certain church, you were shunned and relegated to the fringe of society.

Of course, these people mirrored the actions of the know-it-all Pharisees in Jesus' time. The Pharisees had also deluded themselves into thinking that if they followed certain rules that it would lead them on a straight path to heaven. But 2,000 years is a long time to understand that even people today would believe that they are the sole heirs to heaven because they have the inside track on how to get there. Following the 300+ rules of the Pharisees wouldn't get them to heaven back then and following the exclusive rules of a particular church doctrine won't get you inclusively there now. Yet, despite Jesus alerting the Pharisees about their own egos and the falsehoods of their own doctrine, we still have Pharisees-like people today who proclaim that their church's doctrine has secured for them the only path to heaven.

14. Believe in Jesus' Supernatural Power

"I have been driven many times upon my knees by the overwhelming conviction that I had nowhere else to go." Abraham Lincoln, attributed to Noah Brook (journalist/friend)

Six days before the Feast of the Passover in Bethany and after Jesus had raised Lazarus from the dead, the people visiting for the Passover crowded towards Jesus. But they were crowding towards Jesus to see Lazarus as much as to see Jesus. "… and they came not for Jesus' sake only, but they might see Lazarus also whom he had raised from the dead" (John 12:9). Because of Lazarus' resurrection by Jesus more people believed that Jesus was the Son of God, although many rulers who also believed on Jesus did not confess it because their confession would have gotten them thrown out of the synagogue. It's curious that Lazarus' resurrection created such an increase in believers; Jesus had performed many miracles before, so why did this miracle stimulate such a great interest? The fact that many people could see the miracle of Lazarus being alive when he had been previously dead for 4 days is the key. "Seeing is believing," someone once said. Therefore, because many people could see the miracle of a walking, talking, and breathing Lazarus, it made many more of them believe. For them, faith was not enough; they needed to see a concrete miracle performed by Jesus with their own eyes, and Lazarus provided them with the concrete proof that they needed.

However, Satan's reaction in the Pharisees' heart to Lazarus—who was once dead for four days in a tomb, and who was now walking proof of Jesus' claim to be the Son of God—imparted a defensive reaction. Instead of marveling at the sight of a once dead Lazarus walking among them, Satan's influence helps the Pharisees to decide that they should not only kill Jesus, the maker of the miracle, but also kill Lazarus, who was the proof of the miracle itself. Once again, even the concrete proof of seeing someone who was dead and now alive will not move the Pharisee's hardened hearts to believe the truth about Jesus, and you can thank Satan for that disbelief. The fact that the Pharisee were now thinking about killing the product of the miracle in Lazarus makes the Pharisee perspective even more satanic. For, the cover-up involving Jesus' identity now expanded to killing those who have experienced the supernatural power of Jesus. Before, those people who had experienced it—like the blind man who received his sight and those close friends and relatives around him—were threatened with only being thrown out of the synagogue. Granted, being thrown out of the synagogue for confessing that Jesus was the Son of God was a harsh punishment, and no one wanted to endure the social stigma of it. But now, Lazarus who was healed from death by Jesus' supernatural power was now being threatened with death by the Pharisee. So, it appears that as the miracles of Jesus have expanded from healing the blind to raising the dead that Satan's power over the Pharisees has also increased from their punishment for confessing that Jesus is the Son of God and being ejected from the synagogue to being ejected from life.

Therefore, as more and more people believed in Jesus because of Jesus' supernatural power and as Jesus' miracles increased in power to raising the dead to life, the "… chief priests consulted that they might put Lazarus also to death" (John 12:10). Thus, Satan's grand cover-up through the Pharisees to deny the identity of Jesus continued. They must have really loved Satan's benefit of high religious social status to turn their heads away from the miracle of Lazarus. If the miracle of seeing a once dead and now a come back to life Lazarus wouldn't convince them of Jesus' identity, it's evident that Satan had a firm grasp on them and that nothing would.

On a personal note, there was a time before my salvation where I had reached the lowest moral point in my life. I was around thirty years of age and was still clueless about Jesus, redemption, and salvation. Therefore, all my actions were self-serving and being directed by Satan. However, I somehow knew that I was not living up to my own expectations for myself and that I had, indeed, reached rock bottom. Then, one night at the lowest point of my life, I was visited by the supernatural power of Jesus. In one short dream, I was first visited by Satan, who appeared as an undulating turmoil of blue goo that passed slowly in front of me from left to right. And while I watched Satan as writhing blue goo pass in front of me, a deep sense of dread filled my heart. Then after Satan had disappeared on my right, an image of Jesus Christ appeared on my left, and Jesus was floating gracefully in mid-air while carrying my heart in front of Him in His cupped hands, and I immediately felt the greatest sense of peace in my life. I knew then that Jesus was presenting me with a choice about how to live my life: I could continue following in the dreadful feelings of Satan or I could follow in the peace and tranquility found in Jesus Christ. Thus, a one-minute dream as a supernatural vision from Jesus Christ changed my life. And since then, I have read numerous articles about people who have also seen Satan in a dream and he always appeared as a dreadful, undulating mass of blue goo.

15. Spread the Good News

"All I have seen teaches me to trust the Creator for all I have not seen."
—Ralph Waldo Emerson

In Acts 16:16-18 when a vision appeared to Paul and he went to Macedonia to preach and spread the gospel, he and other disciples encountered "… a certain damsel possessed with a spirit of divination met us, which brought her masters much gain by soothsaying" (Acts 16:16). The word divination means "To practice to fore tell future events or discover hidden knowledge by occult or supernatural means" (Random House Webster College Dictionary). Therefore, a woman possessed by an occult spirit who used this spirit to make money for her master followed Paul for days crying aloud, "… these men are the servants of the most high God, which shew unto us the way of salvation "(Acts 16:17). So, this woman followed Paul for days and was a town crier who announced Paul and the disciples' presence and mission. Paul didn't cast the evil spirit out of the woman immediately because he probably assumed that she was harmless. But then, after days of her shouting next to him, Paul became annoyed by her overt and loud proclamations and one day he simply could not tolerate her shouting any more. So, he stopped her shouting and commanded that the evil spirit within her to come out. "And this did she many days. But Paul, being grieved, turned and said to the spirit, I command thee in the name of Jesus Christ to come out of her. And he came out the same hour" (Acts 16:18).

This incident with the shouting woman and Paul's growing frustration with her reminds me of a man who preaches the gospel every Saturday morning over a microphone and a loudspeaker attached to his chest at the local downtown Farmer's Market. While the man's intentions at first seem good for spreading the gospel by getting people to at least hear it, the man's electronic speaker approach grated on people's nerves after a while to the point where they become annoyed like Paul. Of course, the woman in Paul's case was motivated by an occult spirit (i.e., Satan), while the man blaring the gospel at Farmer's Market may have been a sincere Christian, while his method of delivery—the electronic microphone and speaker—might have been his biggest problem.

How to spread and deliver the "Good News" of Jesus to other people is always a balancing act between getting them to listen and offending them to the point where Satan enters them, and they don't listen. I never approached the man at Farmer's Market to see if he was soliciting money for his efforts—like the woman in Paul's time—but his delivery method of the gospel was so annoying that it probably didn't attract listeners to the Word, but probably repelled them. That's the risk a believer takes when initiating dialogue with a non-believer. At Farmer's Market, Satan had made the man blaring the message of salvation appear to be just another "kooky" Christian to people who wanted to enjoy the peace and quiet of choosing fresh vegetables for the week on an early Saturday morning. But the "kooky" Christian wouldn't let them enjoy the peace of a quiet Saturday morning, and the pigeons even departed the moment that the man turned on his amplifier. So, despite the man's good intensions, Satan made his actions counter-productive in getting non-believers to listen to Jesus Christ's message of salvation. He might have been sincere in his efforts, but his delivery played right into Satan's hands by over-whelming rather than engaging the crowd. Therefore, Christians should be aware that—like Paul—that they are combating Satan's influence in both method and message every time they attempt to spread the Word of God and that without the proper method no one will hear the proper message.

16. To Use Non-Violence

"We who engage in nonviolent direct action are not the creators of tension. We merely bring to the surface hidden tension that is already alive." —Martin Luther King

In Genesis 6-8 God decided to end the world with a flood. He does so because of the violence He sees in man. "And God said unto Noah, the end of all flesh is come before me; for the earth is filled with violence through them; and behold, I will destroy them with the earth" (Genesis 6:13). Therefore, God is disappointed with man because of his violent behavior, and He decides to start over again by destroying the earth. Physical violence is Satan's brutish, animalistic behavior reserved for less thoughtful and uncaring people who do not respect the human rights of others. Therefore, even though God put man in charge of all brutish creatures below him on the food chain, God is disappointed that man remains in Satan's beastly state himself.

Because of man's violent behavior, God decides to put an end to all living things on earth, except Noah and his family and all animal species who two by two of male and female gender take refuge on the ark. It should be noted that Noah is not a violent or wicked man, but one who spends his time with the Lord. "... Noah found grace in the eyes of the Lord" (Genesis 6:8).

When the flood waters start to recede, Noah sends out a Dove to take wing from the window of the ark. If the Dove returns, it is because it has not a place on land to rest. "But the dove found no rest for the sole of her foot" (Genesis 8:9). It's interesting that God ended the world because of man's violent nature attributed to Satan, and when Noah wants to see if the water has subsided enough for them to emerge from the ark to a new non-violent world that Noah sends out a Dove—now a symbol of peace—to check whether Satan's influence on earth has ended. Furthermore, when the dove finally returns to the ark with proof that the waters have indeed subsided, the Dove returns with an olive branch—another symbol of peace.

Man must, therefore, restrain himself from his violent and satanic behavior if he wants to be close to God. However, it is difficult for some people to restrain themselves from the anger of Satan's influence, which often leads to the use of violent behavior. But according to God's Word in Genesis 6-8, that is what man should do to reject Satan and to please God. Man must not act out emotionally with violent impulses, for if he does, it only lengthens his own distance from God.

God gave us all a lesson about man's being influenced by Satan when using violent behavior in Genesis when He flooded the earth and killed every living thing because man could not restrain himself from the brutish behavior found in lesser creatures. In fact, evidently man's violent behavior must have been so bad that God chose to save the lives of other lesser creatures by putting them on the ark instead of saving man. Case in point: Why didn't God just destroy all other living creatures and remake them later after the flood? Why did He preserve the life of all other animal species two-by-two by having Noah painstakingly place them on the ark? Perhaps it is a lesson to us that He saved a boatful of lesser species on the ark rather than human beings because they had more value to Him at the time. Evidently, Satan's level of violence in man had exceeded the limits of violence even displayed by wild animals. So, God tames the wild animals two-by-two, has them politely walk into the ark by obediently following His instructions—something that man had not done for quite some time— and He saves them. Hence, on the day(s) when the two-by-two animals filed onto the ark, God saved them to make a point. Because of his violence and Satan's influence, man had become lesser in the eyes of God than those wild animals that He saved on the ark. Yes, that's right!

God had become so disillusioned with man's violent behavior that He chose to book passage for animals instead of us.

17. Practice Christian Charity

"A bone to the dog is not charity. Charity is the bone shared with the dog, when you are just as hungry as the dog." —Jack London

Romans 12:17 states, "Recompense to no man evil for evil..." and Paul addresses the attitude and demeanor of a Christian's behavior, and what Jesus expects from a Christian. As stated by Paul, Christian behavior is the opposite of unchristian behavior, as seen every day in Satan's world. For example, Christians are not to seek revenge upon another person for having been wronged by them. In fact, it is not a Christian's responsibility to seek justice in the world because it is God's role to exact justice. "Vengeance is mine, I will repay, saith the Lord" (Romans 12:19). Therefore, good Christian behavior doesn't seek revenge because God will someday repay those people who hurt Christians. However, not only is a Christian not to seek revenge, but a Christian is also expected to do his utmost to live peaceably with those people who have hurt him. "If it be possible, as much as lieth in you, live peaceably with all men" (Romans 12:18). By doing so, a Christian will set an example for an unbeliever to follow. Truly, Satan's fallen world is filled with hateful people who know not the Lord in their heart, nor God in their soul. These residents who embrace Satan's fallen world are clueless about Jesus, their Holy Spirt, and God's role for them. Instead, they live in the moral vacuum prevalent in Satan's world and will: lie, cheat, and steal without hesitation, blaspheme the Lord Jesus, and contaminate the Holy Spirit with their vile thought and behavior, all the while accepting those amoral traits of Satan as valuable and just.

For instance, many years ago when I was an undergraduate student, young people—at the tender age of 18 years old—had already bought-in to the lies of the Satan, and they would do or say anything to advanced their own agenda, no matter how much it hurt someone else. Case in point. On Sunday nights in the college dormitory, dinner was not served in the cafeteria, so every student was on their own to find other sources of food for the evening. Those students who came from well-to-do families often went out together for Sunday dinner or ordered in pizza to be delivered in the dormitory. I never had any money in college, much less extra money for a Sunday night meal, so I went hungry and would sit around in my dormitory room watching other students eat delivered pizza and submarine sandwiches while pretending not to be hungry. Even when they offered me a slice of pizza, I would refuse it out of pride. Then, one stormy winter night, with the snow furiously falling, and the wind blowing at 35 miles per hour, I was offered a deal for Sunday dinner that I couldn't refuse. Another student wanted a Big Mac and French fries from the McDonald's located two miles away from the dormitory. The blizzard was so bad that cars could not move in it, so he made me the following meal proposition: If I would walk and accompany him to McDonald's through the monster snowstorm, then he would buy me a Big Mac and French fries, too. It seemed to me like a fair trade; I'd keep him company and endure the walk in the storm with him, and then he would reward me with dinner.

So, I accepted his offer and accompanied him on the two-mile trek to McDonald's. Once inside McDonald's, and after an arduous winter journey, I was very hungry and cold; the two-mile walk through the blizzard had not been an easy one. As I approached the counter to order, I noticed that the floors inside McDonald's were wet and covered with black slush, so I was careful not to slip and fall. My blizzard buddy ordered first, and then it was my turn to order, so I started to order my meal when I was abruptly interrupted by my walking companion. "I thought you said that you didn't have any money?" He asked. "I don't. But you said that if I walked with you through the blizzard to McDonald's that you would buy me a Big Mac and fries." To which he responded, "I never said that!" We stared into each other's eyes for a moment; then, it became clear that he had never intended to honor his part of our agreement; he just wanted my protection to walk with him through the snowstorm. So, I slowly turned and walked myself back outside and into awaiting darkness, where I trudged alone another two miles back through the blizzard to the dormitory.

After being lied to, I never spoke to that student again, which somehow provided me with some consolation. But according to Romans 12:20, my behavior was unchristian. Instead of shunning him, I should have spoken to him the next day as if nothing had happened. In fact, I should have bought him dinner on the following Sunday evening. "Therefore, if thine enemy hunger, feed him; if he thirst, give him drink: For in doing so thou shalt heap coals of fire on his head" (Romans 12:20). By giving him Christian charity, the unbeliever—who is quick to use Satan's tools—might see the error of his ways. If not, his continued evil behavior—despite being shown Christ's way—will continue to displease God and thereby widen the gap between them. "Be not overcome of evil but overcome evil with good" (Romans 12:21).

18. Avoid Unchristian Behavior

"One Cardinal entered his cathedral for the first time at his funeral." Barbara Tuchman, The March of Folly

In 1 Corinthians 5, Paul—in his letter to Corinthians—warns them not to associate with people who might believe in Christ but do not behave like Christians. If you fraternize with people of ungodly behavior, then you run the risk of being contaminated by that bad behavior yourself. "Know ye not that a little leaven leaveneth the whole lump" (1 Corinthians 5:6). In other words, a person who is tainted by displaying bad behavior can eventually also spoil everyone associated with him. It goes beyond guilt by association; it is guilt by corruption as Satan's corrupt person spreads their behavior to others. Many times, when a Christian intends to help another person to find Jesus because they can see Satan's workmanship in the person's behavior, the Christian is often led astray by Satan's influence in the corrupt person as well. Therefore, Paul warns Christians to just stay away from and not to associate with corrupt people, lest their corruption spoil them, too.

I grew up in a lower, middle-class neighborhood in Michigan, one that was bordered by lower economic class neighborhoods. From an early age, I was told by my mother not to walk on certain streets because it was unsafe. However, I also went to elementary school with many of the students from those neighborhoods, and from the sixth grade forward, I could see violent behavior and anti-social components in some students' personalities that even at an early age made them penitentiary bound. They wouldn't listen to the good advice of teachers, disregarded the rules, and disrespected others. Thus, even at the young age of eight years, I had recognized people who were not healthy to be around. Eventually, most of the malcontents did go the prison for burglary, drugs, and for being AWOL from the US Army, and I might have been going there too, if I had associated with them. Other students who associated with them because they thought that their disobedient behavior was "cool" also got into trouble with the law with them.

Therefore, Paul identifies some of the bad behaviors exhibited by Satan's influence in an unchristian person. In this way, Paul identifies for a Christian what ungodly behaviors to avoid. "But now, I have written unto you not to keep company, if any man that is called a brother be a fornicator, or covetous, or an idolater, or a railer, or a drunkard, or an extortioner; with such a one no not to eat" (1 Corinthians 5:11). Therefore, a person cannot be a Christian or be called a brother in Christ who does the following things, so don't associate with them. People, who call themselves Christians cannot be: "fornicators," that is sexually immoral; "covetous," that is desirous of wealth and possessions because their heart is worldly and not heavenly; or be an "idolater," that is a worshipper of worldly things instead of God; or a "railer," someone who likes to drink alcohol to excess, or an "extortioner," someone who obtains something by lies, aggression, or force. These types of behaviors, Paul states, are unchristian behaviors, and people who do them should be avoided.

According to Paul, a Christian should not associate with these corrupt people because sooner or later, God will judge them. "Therefore, put away from among yourselves that wicked person" (1 Corinthians 5:13). Subsequently, Paul's letter to the Corinthians is really instruction on basic Christian behavior. If you want to be a Christian, says Paul, then act like one, and avoid Satan, which is still good advice today for any Christian.

19. Trust in God and His Son Jesus

"Pray, and let God worry." – Martin Luther

In 2 Corinthians 1 Paul writes to the Christians at Corinth about the troubles he encountered in Asia because of his preaching the Gospel of Jesus Christ. In doing so, Paul used a unique description of these troubles and how he responded to them. He said that we had "… the sentence of death in ourselves, that we should not trust in ourselves, but in God which raiseth the dead" (2 Corinthians 1:9). Evidently, the troubles encountered by Paul were so massive that he and his companions were overwhelmed and had given their problems over to God to solve.

In normal, everyday life, we pray to God for help in many things, but we do what we can as human beings knowing that God's help is essential for a successful conclusion. I pray every day and throughout the day for the Lord's guidance. I once read an article that stated that most elderly men die in the early morning hours before 6 am. Therefore, every morning when I awaken after 6 am, I thank the Lord for being alive to greet another day. I thank Him for my salvation, which is the greatest gift that anyone can ever receive. I thank Him for knowing that my soul is saved after my physical death and that I will be going to live in heaven with Jesus for eternity. It's a wonderful feeling not to fear your own death, which is the greatest sin, because you already know the spiritual outcome of your holy self. However, there are times when circumstances become so severe—like in Paul's case—when only God can solve the problem and you must put your life entirely into His hands. Ask any soldier about death's randomness in combat. Why did he live and someone standing next to him die, and he will credit his life to the saving grace of God.

So, too, Paul and his companions must have reached that point where their human limitations brought them to the end of the road, and they knew that only God could save them. They were all walking with a "sentence of death" within themselves because they had nothing left to lose. Again, soldiers in combat often reach this same point where they have nothing left to lose and accept that they are going to die. They, like Paul, have concluded that death awaits them and that it's just a matter of time. However, once they accept their impending death and give the burden over to God, the burden of dying is suddenly lifted; now God is the one who will decide, and by no longer trusting in themselves but in Him, they feel relieved.

Yet, with each passing day that combat soldiers remain alive and they get closer to going home, they once again begin to feel the weight of carrying around the responsibility for their own safety. The unthinkable—staying alive and going home—now re-enters their mind, and again the burden returns to them. In a soldiers' case, they once again remember the faces of their love ones back home, and in Paul's case he once again remembered the faces of his fellow Christians in Corinth. Two soldiers with "tombstones in their eyes"—one for God and another for country—trusting in God's grace to save them.

Thus, we must not trust in ourselves as stated in 2 Corinthians 1:9, but trust in God to deliver us from our troubles, no matter how difficult. In the case of Paul, his living through the experience made him reference the grace of God "... which raiseth the dead" (2 Corinthians 9:1) because for him he had come back from the living dead and he knew that only God could have saved him.

20. To Do Good Works with Charity

"The life of a man consists not in seeing visions and in dreaming dreams, but in active charity and in willing service." – Henry Wadsworth Longfellow

First Corinthians 13 addresses the value of charity in one's life. You can seemingly do many Christian works in your life, but if you do them without charity in your heart, then you do them for the wrong reasons. Thus, not the act itself but the motivation—charity—is what's important. "And though I bestow all my goods to feed the poor, and though I give my body to be burned, and have not charity, it profiteth me nothing" (1 Corinthians 13:3). Therefore, without a pure heart of charity that reflects the honesty of the action, the action becomes only a fraction of itself because it was done for twisted reasons. Some of these reasons might be the ego's quest for self-satisfaction or for greed. Regardless of reason, if an ulterior motive exists, the action itself lacks purity and is reduced. "Charity suffereth long and is kind; charity envieth not; charity vaunteth not itself, is not puffed up..." (1 Corinthians 13:4). Hence, charity—and the pure unselfish application of it—becomes greater than the action itself because the act will be impure without the component of unselfish charity and the genuineness as the reason for the action.

When I was in high school nearing the Christmas season, my high school took up a collection of can goods to be distributed to people in need at Christmas. On the surface, it looked like a good and charitable thing to do. However, the students from rich families turned the event into a competition about which can-goods team could bring in the most cans. With this competition mindset, the primary concern of helping needy families was lost. Now, the event became more about the people who were collecting the cans and less about the people who would be receiving them. Therefore, the purpose for the event itself was lost in the zeal of competition.

Furthermore, after all the cans goods were collected and the winning team of the can goods competition was announced, no student from a rich family ever wanted to distribute the can goods to needy families. They did not want to go into the poorer neighborhoods to see the faces of the people for whom they had collected the cans. So, every year five guys – including me – from working class neighborhoods would visit and distribute the can goods to the families in need. When I distributed the can goods to poorer families, I learned a lot about life and about how grateful I was to my parents for providing me with a stable home environment. My father worked on a factory assembly line for over 40 years, and my mother worked at odd jobs to make financial ends meet. One Christmas Season after an eye-opening can delivering experience at one house, I came home and thanked them for providing me with a good home.

Therefore, out of the purity of the heart from which charity is given, and when behavior stems from this pure behavior, then the behavior is also pure and whole. "Doth not behave itself unseemly, seeketh not her own, is not easily provoked, thinkest no evil" (1Corinthians 13:5). When behavior is done with a pure and charitable heart then all things become possible and the power of the act becomes unlimited. And when the act is performed through charity of heart, then the actions are also whole and truthful. For truth through genuine charity, because of its unlimited power and its truthfulness, can "Beareth all things, believeth all things, hopeth all things, endureth all things" (1 Corinthians 13:7). However, when good acts are done without the purity of heart of charity, then Satan is at work and things will not be whole and will fail. "Charity never faileth: but whether there be prophecies, they shall fail; whether there be tongues, they shall cease; whether there be knowledge, it shall vanish away" (1 Corinthians 13:8). Thus, no matter how great the act, it will be diminished without the part that charity plays in giving it.

However, as mortals for the time being, it is often difficult to understand where someone's ego stops in the heart and where genuine charity begins. People cannot often distinguish between the two because we live in Satan's fallen world where we will never be able to totally discern the complete truth. Therefore, people's vision in a fallen world is obscured by Satan's evil environment and their fallibility in it. The result is that we will never completely be able to understand our own actions and the wholeness and genuine quality of charity in them. By not being able to do so, this results in our inability to totally discern and understand our own actions and their motives. This lack of untainted and clarity of vision on earth, however, will someday gave way to the total truth where every puzzle piece of life fits and is understood in heaven. "For now we see through a glass, darkly: but then face to face: Now I know in part; but then shall I know even as also I am known" (1 Corinthians 13:12). Therefore, we will someday be in heaven and know ourselves totally and our motivations fully, and what it meant to the totality of our heart's spiritual experience when we someday meet God. Only He knows us totally. But for now, we can read the Bible for advice and learn from it, in hopes of becoming a better person with pure intentions with our Christian actions being as honest and performed from the heart as much as humanly possible. In this regard, 1 Corinthians 13:13 gives us good advice on how to proceed in our lives as Christians: "And now abideth faith, hope, and charity, these three; but the greatest of these is charity."

21. To Be Generous

"You give little when you give of your possessions. It is when you give of yourself that you truly give." —Kahlil Gibran, The Prophet

In 2 Corinthians 9:7, Paul states that "God loves a cheerful giver." In other words, God loves those people who give freely out of the abundance of their heart. No one is making them give to God; they do it because they are glad to. This verse is most referenced in terms of giving money to the church—that people should not only be willing, but happy, to put their money into the offering plate. Yet, the term "giver" can mean many things besides the giving of your treasure (money). For instance, there is also the giving of your time, which in many instances is sometimes more often necessary than money.

Time is your only personal, non-renewable resource; you can always earn more money, but you cannot earn one more second of time. We are only allotted by God so much time on earth. Then, that is it. There are not any extensions. In many ways, time is an unmanageable resource because we never know how much is in the bank. Unlike a bank account, where you can watch your money deplete or grow and know how much is left and how long it will last, your time on earth is unknown and incalculable because you never know how much time is left in your life's account. You can plan on being alive in the future by scheduling events, but there is no guarantee that you will be alive to attend them. That's why volunteering your time is so important because you are donating a personal resource over which you have no control. It is giving something of yourself that only God knows how much you have left. Therefore, a trust exists between God and a Christian giver when he commits his resource of time.

Another type of giving is the giving of your heart. The giving of your heart is a gift from your spiritual self so that you are not only volunteering your physical presence but also your heart's presence as well. For instance, tossing money into an offering plate at church and then feeling proud about yourself for doing so is only a first-step Christian's response to his obligation to the church. It is true that money makes most things move, but to be involved emotionally in a church, you must care about the spiritual health of the congregation. At many times a church can be monetarily healthy but spiritually bankrupt. In a spiritually bankrupt church, gossip and in-fighting prevail and are deemed normal, while Christian charity takes a backseat to personal ambitions and power to drive the agenda. In fact, I've known pastors who when influenced by Satan have depleted the Christian will of their own congregations by imposing church rules of manipulation and control. In some cases, these pastors exerted so much control over church members that it extended beyond scriptural basis and into demanding unchristian practices.

I knew a pastor and his wife who exerted overwhelming manipulation and control over their small church congregation. Their power extended well beyond the walls of the church and into the living room of church members. No one could date without first getting the blessing of the pastor and his wife. No one could get married unless the couple and the union was okayed by the pastor, and church members (i.e., spies) were encouraged to "narc" on other church members. The pastor and his wife controlled who married whom, and infractions like holding hands with someone other than okayed by the pastor resulted in getting "churched," that is brought before the entire congregation to be ridiculed. Church members were only allowed to speak to other church members, and church was held seven nights per week. In short, the pastor and his wife used the church as an instrument of power to control and manipulate their congregation.

So, it is every Christian's responsibility to regularly check the spiritual pulse of the church congregation to make sure its spiritual vital signs are strong. By doing so, each Christian lends his spiritual self to the good of the entire church body. "For where two or three are gathered together in my name, there am I in the midst of them" (Matthew 18:20).

22. Fear God's Power

"Your mistake is that you don't know the Scriptures, and you don't know the power of God." – Jesus (Matthew 22:29)

In Exodus 7-11, when Moses and Aaron asked for the release of the Israelites from Egypt and from slavery by the Pharaoh, God sets upon Egypt a series of plagues to eventually soften the Pharaoh's heart. The Pharaoh must have mistakenly believed in his own deity because he rejects God many times despite Egypt being repeatedly punished by God. Plagues of many kinds beset Egypt like locusts, frogs, hail, and fire. Yet, the Pharaoh refused to let the Israelites leave Egypt. The Pharaoh knew that he wouldn't be able to accomplish his secular plans without the help of slave labor, so it appears that the Pharaoh's truculence was due more to how the exodus of the Israelites would influence Egypt's secular economic condition rather than its spiritual one. Thus, the Pharaoh's secular power vs God's supernatural power are pitted against each other. The battle, of course, is terribly lopsided; God is all powerful, while the Pharaoh's power is limited to his humanness. Thus, it was never a battle to be won by the Pharaoh, and it was always a battle within the Pharaoh as to when he would give in and let the Israelites leave Egypt.

While the various plagues brought down upon Egypt by God are frightening, I found the power of the plague of darkness to be the most convincing. Imagine, living in a world where darkness surrounds everything 24/7 except in the houses of the people of Israel. "And Moses stretched forth his hand toward heaven; and there was a thick darkness in all the land of Egypt three days. They saw not one another; neither rose from his place for three days: all the children of Israel had light in their dwellings" (Exodus 10:22-23). Today, imagine the force of a hurricane's winds destroying everything in its path, and the electrical power grid being destroyed and darkness prevailing. Yet, despite the hurricane's downing of the power lines, the hurricane's winds and darkness does not touch the homes of all saved Christians, and a bright light still shines in their homes. While everyone outside stands in Satan's darkness, those special people inside are untouched and bathed in God's supernatural light.

From a metaphorical perspective, the houses being filled with the Lord's light in Exodus 10 could represent those Christians today who stand in salvation's light in Satan's darkened and alien world. "… among whom ye shine as lights in the world" (Philippians 2:15). It's obvious from the light shining only from the houses of the Israelites that God has set them apart as protected people, just like Jesus has set apart His known sheep as saved people since the foundation of the world. However, today Satan's darkness has blinded many more people, and as they stumble blindly around in their everyday world`, they embrace darkness as if it were light. And they, like the Pharaoh, continue to resist God. Fortunately, by Jesus dying on the cross for our sins and then being resurrected, He has become the world's supernatural light, and by shining light on His resurrection and on His gift of salvation, Christians today can extend God's supernatural light into the dark places of their own lives with the same eternal glow that filled the Israelites' houses.

23. Don't Backslide into Sin

"A man who gives in to temptation after five minutes simply does not know what it would have been like an hour later." CS Lewis, Mere Christianity

Paul in 2 Corinthians 12:20 speaks to the people of Corinth about how fearful he is that they have not repented and have retained their old sinful behavior. Paul is planning to visit Corinth and he doesn't want to find them in their previous sinful condition. So, before his arrival there, he writes to them to hold them accountable for their behavior. "For I fear, lest, when I come, I shall not find you such as I would…" (2 Corinthians 12:20). Being held accountable for your actions in anything is good. Without accountability regarding the outcome, one cannot measure what progress has been made and that was Paul's intent. He wanted to let the people of Corinth know before his arrival that upon his arrival that he was doing an assessment of their Christian progress by measuring the absence of—or presence of—sinful behavior. Paul knows how they behaved before, and now he wants to see how they behave now—after he had previously introduced them to the gospel of

Jesus Christ.

This is an important lesson for us all. For, has our behavior changed for the better since we have come to know Christ? Or, has Satan crept back into our behavior to renew bad habits? Or, worse yet, has our behavior dramatically worsened? Being changed from the heart-side out by the revelation of salvation by Jesus Christ should provide you with putting on a new personal Christian identity, and this Christian identity should be evident to you and to others as evidence by your Christian behavior. "Therefore, if any man be in Christ, he is a new creature: old things are passed away; behold, all things are become new" (2 Corinthians 5:17). If not, as feared by Paul at Corinth, then the conversion to Christ wasn't real, and you have not felt the necessity of changing your behavior upon being saved.

It is always a constant and headlong battle to pray for the conversion of your previous self into a new creature of God, one saved from the horrid events of the world because of your planned placement into the house of the Lord upon your death. Yet, no one's behavior is perfect, and we are all tempted by Satan, and sometimes Christians fall—yet get back up again. Sometimes I believe that Christians fall because it is a reminder that no matter how hard they try that they still need the forgiving strength and grace of the Lord Jesus Christ. Jesus doesn't orchestrate the fall, yet it is certainly a reminder that we mortals do, indeed, need Jesus as our savior. Every Christian knows when he falls short of himself that he becomes convicted by the Holy Spirit for his shortcomings. Then, the guilt starts and the remorse of having fallen. But the good news is that once a Christian is saved that he is always saved. Thus, no matter how hard you fall, you will still be embraced by Jesus when you try to get back up. However, I wouldn't constantly fall anticipating the generosity of Christ to save you once again just because you took advantage of your saved status. If you tempt God to get bailed out again in this scenario, you just might be surprised to find out that you were not saved in the first place.

"Accountability" is the key word. In Corinth's case, Paul is doing the assessment to hold the people of Corinth up to the behavior befitting of a follower of Jesus Christ, and he does so by specifically listing previous behaviors that were noted on his previous visit, and if these behaviors persist, then little or no Christian progress has been made.

"… lest there be debates, envyings, wraths, strifes, backbitings, whisperings, swelling, tumults:…" (2 Corinthians 12:20). Therefore, the items on Paul's list specially state the behaviors at Corinth that he perceived previously that were unbecoming of a Christian. If you examine the list, all the specific items relate to the discord among people. While the items might allude to personal behavior, such negative and sinful personal behavior by some can negatively influence and reduce the solidarity of all. The items listed all have a deceitful and dishonest quality about them, as one individual relates to another. "Debates" (i.e., arguments) among members of the congregation should not exist, as well as "envyings" (i.e., jealousy). "Wraths" (i.e., anger) should not exist, and "stifes," (i.e., bitterness and competition) should also not exist. "Backbiting"—that is, attacking the character of another person in their absence, and "whisperings" (i.e., gossip) should not exist. "Swellings" (i.e., ego tripping) and "tumults" (i.e., commotion) should also not exist. In short, Paul has heard that there is a general discord among the Christians at Corinth, and he doesn't want to see any of the behavioral items on his list being done.

So, who in a Christian congregation today is responsible to cease sinful behavior from its members? Obviously, it's the obligation of the church hierarchy, yet isn't it the obligation of every Christian brother and sister? Only Jesus can make people aware of their sinfulness by working on a person's heart, but fellow Christians can support Jesus' efforts by exercising their Christian responsibility to hold other Christians accountable. In 2 Corinthians 12:20, it appears that Paul suspects that he isn't going to like what he sees from the Christians in Corinth, and he gives them a warning—a heads up—before his arrival that they still have time to act like a Christian congregation. It's a good lesson for all Christians in any century.

24. Believe in Your Holiness

"People have no idea what one saint can do: for sanctity is stronger than the whole of hell." Thomas Merton, Seven Story Mountain

If you do not believe in God and in His Son Jesus Christ and you do not believe in the Holy Spirit, then in your ignorance you will suffer the wrath of God through our Lord Jesus when He returns. In this regard, the fire and brimstone preachers had it right about those people who don't believe. "And to you who are troubled rest with us, when the Lord

Jesus shall be revealed from heaven with his mighty angels, In flaming fire taking vengeance on them that know not God, and that obey not the gospel of our Lord Jesus Christ:" (2 Thessalonians 7-8). Therefore, if you're a nonbeliever, then there is, indeed, something to worry about.

For example, the scientific The Theory of Evolution reduces man to just another species that developed over time after climbing out of the slime of a swamp. This makes human development no more than arbitrary where gene mutations over time established everything from the way we think to the way we mate. In Evolutionary Theory terms, a family then becomes nothing more than a breeding unit where genes are spliced with another breeding unit's genes, and where genetics become more important than laughter. To me, this approach to understanding the start of human existence is a grim one, for it leaves everything up to chance. Human beings will become what human beings will become based on genetic mutations. We will be ourselves because of random occurrence, and for a species that prides itself on the precise calculation of scientific data, it strikes me as ironic that non-believers accept the fact that their own creation occurred by random chance.

While scientists try to calculate and analyze everything else on earth so precisely, they still believe that human beings were solely created by an out-of-control evolutionary process? A more reasonable explanation for a scientist's calculating finite equations to explain our existence in the world would be that a finite application by God had already been applied to the world in the first place, and that He has hot-wired us to do our mortal inferior best to try and understand it. Such interconnectedness displayed in all species in the world should be a scientist's first clue that such precision could not have taken place randomly by evolution; it had to be created by the design of a more powerful Deity who carefully crafted each species on the earth to act and counteract to balance nature into one harmonious equation. Yet, science still believes in its own judgement about how the earth and its species began. According to science, we—like everything else on earth—are just one big mistake multiplied by many little mistakes (mutations) that took place over billions of years that precisely pieced us together.

From a Creationist Theory standpoint, the precisely pieced puzzle to the start of our human existence did not occur randomly, and to believe that it did takes an imagination far greater than it takes to believe that God created us. That's right! It takes more imaginative effort to believe in how all of evolution took place randomly to such an exact extent than it takes to have faith that God created it! However, in the studies of science, faith is not in the equation; empirical evidence is always necessary. For a scientist, seeing is believing, and if you can't prove it through the human senses, then it doesn't exist, even though all the evidence of God's elaborate and finite results in the world suggests that the creation evidence is right before everyone's eyes. The conclusion of how and why we exist and why heaven and earth were created for us by God is incomprehensible to man, which suggests that either random mutations still exceed the understanding by man's intelligence or that a more intelligent Being created it all.

25. Discern Evil

"Better shun the bait, than struggle in the snare." —John Dryden, Marriage A La Mode

Almost every day in the media, I hear some comment made about those crazy evangelical Christians. But in 2 Timothy 1:7, scripture makes it clear who is crazy and who is not. In 2 Timothy 1:7, Paul states, "For God hath not given us the spirit of fear; but of power, and of love, and of a sound mind." So, faith in Jesus Christ provides Christians not only with power and love, but it also provides them with the power of a sound mind. Therefore, if a Christian has a sound mind, then what kind of mind must a non-Christian have who criticizes a Christian? You get the point: In Satan's fallen world you can expect most people to be fallen. Uprightness of character is not one of Satan's redeeming qualities, and as long as Satan can convince people that right is wrong and that wrong it right, people living in a fallen world will respect the wrong things and disrespect the right ones.

For instance, in a fallen world Satan will say that abortion is right—that killing innocent babies is okay to do. And some people—because of Satan's influence—believe that to be true. But how can murdering babies alive in their mother's womb be okay? Aren't there better and more humane ways of approaching the issue than killing the innocent? Why punish the innocent people for behavior that they didn't do? I can't imagine how doctors—people who take the Hippocratic Oath to do no harm – can extract a human life from its mother's womb and kill it. I guess sometimes the evidence proves that Satan's domain is an uncivilized and primitive world where pagan rituals are still performed. Every day, unborn babies are sacrificed to the gods of expediency, selfishness, and convenience, and Satan wants you to believe that it is your self-serving privilege to kill them. Abortion is a demonic and pagan act. In fact, no other human act states more overtly the hideous presence of Satan's influence in the world where wrong is deemed right. Life is sacred, and it can be given and only taken by God. And life is life—no matter the age.

26. Know Your Skills Come from God

"All of my writing is God-given." —Ray Bradbury

When God was appointing Moses in Exodus 35 to deliver a message to the people of Israel about how to build His tabernacle, God specifically called out one person to be involved in the tabernacle's construction. "I have called by name Bezaleel the son of Uri, the son of Hur, of the tribe of Judah. I have filled him with the spirit of God, in wisdom, and in understanding, and in knowledge, and in all manner of workmanship" (Exodus 35:2-3). If anyone ever wondered about the origins of their skill sets in the workplace, Exodus 35:2-3 makes it clear that your skills and aptitudes in life spring from God. God gives you your skill sets, just like He imparted them to Bezaleel to make His tabernacle. Whether God had given these skill sets to Bezaleel previously or he woke up one morning a genius, we don't know. But one thing is for sure, if God wrote a letter of recommendation for Bezaleel, you know that he was the front-runner for the job. And that's the way God wanted it; He wanted us to recognize the inherent value found in the skill sets in every human being. I don't know about you, but I often marvel at the magnificent work being done by others. Think about all the intricate work of carpenters, mechanics, artists, and painters—of teachers, politicians, and writers. Every job has value according to God, or else He wouldn't have created all the different skill sets necessary to do them.

I have often wondered why I could write and teach writing yet couldn't lay cement or hang dry wall? The answer is because God gave me my skill sets, just like He gave you your skill sets. We can't know how to do everything ourselves and that makes us dependent on others. "Bear ye one another's burdens, and so fulfil the law of Christ" (Galatians

6:2). When students tell me that they don't know what they want to study for a career, I usually tell them to think about what they like to do in their spare time. What activities people gravitate towards in their spare time is often related to their aptitude for using skill sets that can often be an indicator for a career.

Because God created so many people with different skill sets, we should be grateful that those people exist. The key world is "grateful." However, instead of being grateful for other people being able to do something that we can't, Satan makes many people become jealous of them. This is Satan's way of turning right thinking into wrong thinking. Not many people are so multi-talented that they can do everything at the highest level. The exception to this scenario was probably Bezaleel whose contribution to building God's tabernacle included: working in gold, silver, and brass; cutting stones and setting them; and carving timber. Nonetheless, God also assigned "Aholiab, from the tribe of Dan, to make the furniture, candlesticks, incense, cloths, and anointing oil" (Exodus 31:6-11). Therefore, while Bezaleel could work in many areas of the Tabernacle, he still could not work in all of them. He needed the help of Aholiab to get the job done. Furthermore, these two men called out by God were supported by other people whose hearts were wise "…that they may make all that I have commanded thee" (Exodus 31:6). The building of God's tabernacle was a group effort with everyone supplying their own "God-given" talent. They didn't argue over their skill sets; they didn't pretend that they had skills sets that they didn't. They worked together with each contributing what skill God had given them to complete the task.

In Satan's fallen world, this cooperation among many people today is rare because everyone wants to be the boss, regardless of whether they have the requisite skill sets. There's nothing worse in the workplace than a boss who has never performed their subordinates' jobs and doesn't have the skill sets required of them, yet this person evaluates their subordinates job performance. So, the take-away point from Exodus 31 is that God gives us our skill sets and our aptitude for them. Many people, however, want to drift away from their God-given talents in favor of pursuing another occupation. I don't know about you, but I would rather have a heart surgeon operate on me who has a genuine aptitude for it, rather than someone who skipped their God-given skill sets and went to medical school because of the money. In the first instance, God is involved; in the second, Satan.

I once lived next door to a woman who was a nurse but wanted to become surgeon. She had been a nurse for fifteen years, and one day she decided that she wanted to go to Medical School to be a surgeon. The woman was small in stature and quiet, and at first glance I wondered if she had the skill sets to be a good surgeon. Then one day she met a large rattle snake in her front yard while she was walking to her car. The rattle snake was coiled up with its head raised in her driveway. Instead of running the other way, like I would, she calmly walked back to her garage, grabbed a shovel, and chopped off the rattle snake's head. She then skinned the rattle snake with her jack knife and made herself a hatband out of its skin for her straw hat, which she always wore while working in her garden. Like I said: We all have our own skill sets given to us by God and killing and skinning rattle snakes isn't included in mine.

27. Know Moral Behavior Comes from God

"Every good gift comes from above." James 1:17

However, if a good gift exists, then a bad gift must also exist. Yet only the good gift comes from above. Therefore, a bad gift must come from below. And, if a good gift is only given by God, then who gives us a bad gift?

That's right, bad gifts are distributed every day by Satan, who deceives people into thinking that they are receiving good gifts. For instance, being able to politically out-maneuver a fellow employee by taking credit for their work is not a good gift. A fallen world's principles might consider being able to do so a good gift; a world's system controlled by Satan might think that but being able to deceive to compete dishonestly at work is a good gift, but it is not one from God. It is a gift given to you by Satan and puffing up your ego after your deceitful political victory is adding insult to soulful injury. Therefore, there is a difference between what is valuable to God, and what is valuable to a fallen world controlled by Satan, and one should not confuse a good gift given to you for righteous behavior with a bad gift given by Satan for evil behavior. "Love not the world, neither the lust of the flesh, and the lust of the eyes, and the pride of life, is not of the Father, but is of the world" (1 John 2:15). For instance, being able to lie convincingly to someone's face while looking them straight in the eye is not a gift from God; such behavior should not be perceived as a good gift but as a bad gift, a curse—a human flaw—that through prayer should be purged from your personality. But Satan likes you to believe that good is bad and bad is good. So, some people who would rather believe in Satan's wrong-world thinking instead of doing what is right through God's gifts are perpetuating evil in the world.

But God will not give you more than you can handle concerning your weight in the world. So, if you pray to the Lord Jesus for guidance, then you will be able to get out from under the burden of your evil and to cast it aside. However, you must be ready to take Jesus' high road to better moral behavior. To stop evil behavior, your soul must be able and willing to exchange it for good behavior. In other words, you must have a change of heart for goodness to take hold of you over evil. Without an inner soulful willingness to change by turning towards Jesus for direction, then moral behavioral change will not occur.

Many people, however, simply do not want to exchange those bad gifts from Satan for good gifts from God because of Satan's allure of short-termed worldly benefits. Lying by taking credit for someone else's work provides short-term benefits like a promotion or a salary increase. But these benefits are, indeed, only short-termed. One day you will retire from your job and your work world will no longer be relevant to your life; as you grow elderly and suffer the consequences of a failing physical body, the importance of your worldly work will fade. All things pass away, and as your physical life deteriorates and now ponders and intertwines with your spiritual life, you now have a very important question to ask: Do you think of your previous deceitfulness at work as good gift? I hope not because your life of lies in the workplace is abhorrent in the eyes of God. Or should you get down on your knees today and pray to Jesus for forgiveness for all those people you have hurt in your life by deceit? The choice is yours, but you can't have it both ways. "Ye cannot serve God and mammon (money)" (Matthew 6:24). Either you accept your sinful satanic ways as good as judged by Satan's world, or you take responsibility for your deceitful behavior in the workplace for its sinful essence and see how Satan has manipulated you for your entire life. Bad is not good because only "good gifts" come from God.

28. Don't Worship False gods

"Whatever your heart clings to and confides in, that is really your God, your functional savior." —Martin Luther

In Deuteronomy 12:13, it seems that God wants the people of Israel, the people who he has delivered from slavery in Egypt—and the people he has favored—to know and to understand the depth of temptation relative to worshipping other false gods. In doing so, God makes it clear that the temptation to worship false gods is everywhere. In fact, the world seems to be inundated with temptations to worship things other than God. In Deuteronomy 12:13 God states, "Namely, the gods of the people which are round about you, nigh unto thee, or far off from thee, from one end of the earth even unto the other end of the earth." In other words, God warns the people of Israel to be careful because the temptation of false gods is everywhere. It is so pervasive that the temptation to worship other gods is both close to you and all round you, and the temptation is also both far off from you and it extends from one end of the earth to the other end of the earth. In short, you can't escape the temptation of worshipping other gods because they are everywhere, which means that you must be on guard 24/7 and everywhere you go to resist such temptation because it never leaves you." No man can serve two masters: for either he will hate one and love the other; or else he will hold to the one and despise the other. Ye cannot serve God and mammon (i.e., money)" (Matthew 6:24).

When reading this passage, it was as if God had written it for today. Imagine, if God believed that the temptation extended from one end of the earth back then to the other, think about today in the age of the internet and what it has done to make the new gods even more accessible worldwide. Today, it seems that sin—like back then—is everywhere, and as soon as your focus becomes on something else rather than upon worshipping God through His Son Jesus Christ, then your mind has become contaminated by a false god. Today, false gods exist everywhere. Television and movies promote celebrities as false gods and as someone to be worshiped. Car advertisements introduce the latest luxury vehicles as things to be worshipped. Politicians treat their political offices as if their entitled to the office, and that is not owned by the citizens in a democracy. All these examples, and many more, illustrate God's point to the Israelites—that anything that influences your mind away from following God's commandments is a distraction and a temptation of a false god. Back then, the worship of false gods probably occurred because of the shiny gold and silver objects that lured people in by their brightness. Today, it's the shiny new boat or the silver windows of a luxury apartment up in the sky forty-five stories. Yet, the import and allure of these objects and celebrity personalities are no different from worshipping the newest pharaoh chariots back then. Anything that comes between your true spiritual mission on earth given to you by God is a false god: yesterday, today, or tomorrow. "Through thy precepts I get understanding therefore, I hate every false way" (Psalm 119:104). And, only by steering ourselves clear of these types of temptations that remain all around us can we remain grounded with our attention on the one true God who sent His only Son Jesus Christ to save us.

29. Remember, the World is Satan's Unholy Domain

"Awake, arise or be forever fall'n." John Milton, Paradise Lost

In Timothy 3:1, Paul warns Timothy "... that in the last days perilous times shall come." It's interesting that the perilous times found in the last days are not created by God, but by humans. Hence, the peril in the world is manmade, and it is a result of our own disobedience to God. People have created their own perilous condition because their behavior has been to disrespect and disregard God. An outgrowth of people turning their back on God is that humans have drifted away from God's principles of moral behavior found in the Bible. Instead, Satan has ensured that people have chosen to pursue their own ungodly ways. "For men be lovers of their own selves, covetous, boasters, proud, blasphemers, disobedient to parents, unthankful, unholy" (2 timothy 3:2). Therefore, by ignoring God and by pursing their own worldly interests at the direction of Satan, people have turned themselves and their world into something unholy. Their selfishness has created a behavior that contradicts God's ways, and by doing so they have strayed away from God. Now, many people don't love and respect God, but they have instead "... become lovers of their own selves ... without natural affection" (2 Timothy 3:1-2).

The phrase "without natural affection" is particularly important. Because of their inhuman behavior, people have strayed so far from God and His ways that people have left some of their humanness behind. That behavior was previously natural to people, like their affection for others, and it has been replaced by the greed of self-interest where charity is abandoned. Therefore, the human condition now is unnatural to their basic being as once created in them by God because now they are "… despisers of those that are good" (Timothy 3:3).

People have themselves and Satan to blame for their current ungodly condition. And the irony is that while people have strayed far away from God and His affection, they—in their ignorance—believe that they are living the good life. And why wouldn't they believe it? They are not being governed by God's moral principles and they are "… incontinent," that is, lacking self-control. In fact, people are so blinded by their disobedience to God that they believe that their chaotic mess of an existence is a good one. And this brings us back to the principle of Satan making people believe that wrong is right and that bad is good. People's condition is so bad that it is "fierce," which alludes to reverting to a beastly nature.

Thus, people are in an unnatural condition that is "Ever learning, and never able to come to the knowledge of the truth" (2 Timothy 3:7). Despite all of people's worldly knowledge and pursuits, their blindness toward God will never allow them to know the truth about Jesus Christ and salvation. The truth, of course, is that God is in charge, and people should be running towards Him and not away from Him, especially if they have heard the gospel of Jesus Christ, yet choose to ignore it. "All scripture is given by inspiration of God, and is profitable for doctrine, for reproof, for correction, for instruction in righteousness" (2 Timothy 3:16).

The truth about life and how to live it is found in the Bible's scripture. Therefore, how to live a righteous life is explained by God in the Bible, and the Bible's scripture is available for everyone to read. So, either by choosing not to read the Bible, or by having read it and behaving badly anyway, people have created a godless and untruthful world, and it is a very dangerous place—one guided by the evils of Satan.

30. Make Moral Decisions

"You had a choice: you could either strain and look at things that appeared in front of you in a fog, painful as it might be, or you could relax and lose yourself." Ken Kesey, One Flew Over the Cuckoo's Nest

On the night that Judas betrayed Jesus and sought out the chief priests and scribes to make a deal for thirty pieces of silver, Satan entered Judas. "Then entered Satan into Judas…" (Luke 22:3). Therefore, God must watch Satan's movements when he enters people to do evil. So why doesn't God stop people from doing evil, if He knows that Satan has just entered them? Why does God allow evil to happen? First, God is not capable of doing evil, and His message for us is only good. Therefore, God is not an accomplice to doing evil, nothing could be further from the truth. God relies on people to stop evil and Satan's temptations by giving people free will to choose either to do good or to do evil. The good and evil struggle is not within God; it is within us as God and Satan do battle for our souls. We chose which way the battle is going and who is winning by the choices that we make in our lives. We have the freedom to choose to either follow God's path or Satan's path. There isn't a halfway; every decision falls on one side of the aisle or the other. Either we do what's morally right or we do what's morally wrong. No decision is sort of evil and no decision is sort of good. The decision must be a clear-cut choice for all parties involved: God, Satan, and you. Thus, you—by your decision—will be doing most of the heavy lifting and either God or Satan will be on the other end of your burden as you carry it up a steep flight of stairs called life.

The decision-making distinction—that is, whether you chose to team with Satan or team with God—will be revealed at the top of the stairs and at the end of your life. Perpetually joining Team Satan by consistently choosing to ignore God and doing evil will land your soul in hell. And, by perpetually choosing to join Team God and partnering with Jesus and His ways will land you in heaven. Indeed, there is a landing at the top of the stairs, a place where you can finally rest from your earthly burdens. But the landing place at the top of the stairs in heaven and the landing place at the depths of hell are much different. Heaven will be a place of peace and serenity, a place where all those worldly burdens that you were carrying by being trapped in your own human imperfection will be lifted, and the peaceful harmony of joy will fill you as you enter the Kingdom of Heaven to be with Jesus. By contrast, if you follow Satan to the landing place of hell, you will find that your earthly burdens will not be lifted from you. In fact, in hell just the opposite happens. Once you reach hell with Satan, you don't get to put down your burdens; you are given more suffering and burden to carry for eternity. "There is no rest for the wicked" is a popular axiom. No rest means no rest—not in this life or the next, where you will suffer because Satan will not allow you to put down your heavy weight.

The choice is yours to make. Another axiom, "the devil made me do it," is not appropriate for your arrival in hell because the Satan did not make you do it. You made the choice to follow Satan by choosing to do so by your own free will. However, while the devil presents and persuades you with his option, you also have another choice—God's holy path to heaven. Right now, the choice is yours to make in this world. It is not God's choice. It is not Satan's choice. It is Your choice. Remember that, the next time you need to make a moral decision, especially if your burdens in this world seem too heavy.

THE END

Other titles from Higher Ground Books & Media:

Wise Up to Rise Up by Rebecca Benston

Raven Transcending Fear by Terri Kozlowski

For His Eyes Only by John Salmon, Ph.D.

Miracles: I Love Them by Forest Godin

32 Days with Christ's Passion by Mark Etter

Knowing Affliction and Doing Recovery by John Baldasare

Out of Darkness by Stephen Bowman

Man Made by Grace by Willie Deeanjlo White

Healing in God's Power by Yvonne Green

Chronicles of a Spiritual Journey by Stephen Shepherd

The Real Prison Diaries by Judy Frisby

My Name is Sam…And Heaven is Still Shining Through by Joe Siccardi

Add these titles to your collection today!

http://www.highergroundbooksandmedia.com

Do you have a story to tell?

Higher Ground Books & Media is an independent Christian-based publisher specializing in stories of triumph! Our purpose is to empower, inspire, and educate through the sharing of personal experiences.

Please visit our website for our submission guidelines.

http://www.highergroundbooksandmedia.com

www.ingramcontent.com/pod-product-compliance
Lightning Source LLC
Chambersburg PA
CBHW061442040426
42450CB00007B/1171